The Crystal Cage

The Crystal Cage

*Adventures of the Imagination
in the Fiction of*

HENRY JAMES

Daniel J. Schneider

THE REGENTS PRESS OF KANSAS

Lawrence

Copyright © 1978 The Regents Press of Kansas
Printed in the United States of America

Library of Congress Cataloging in Publication Data

Schneider, Daniel J., 1927-
    The crystal cage.
    Bibliography: p.
    Includes index.
    1. James, Henry, 1843-1916—Criticism and
    interpretation. I. Title.
    PS2124.S3   813'.4   77-26894
        ISBN 0-7006-0177-5

Contents

Acknowledgments

My indebtedness to some of the great pioneering critics of James's work and to the students of James's life is profound. Quentin Anderson's *The American Henry James* brought me, after much simmering, to a boil; Leon Edel, Saul Rosenzweig, and F. W. Dupee helped me understand the relationship of James's art to his sense of life; among students of James's technique and of his themes, Joseph Warren Beach, L. C. Knights, Sally Sears, Oscar Cargill, and Dorothea Krook have done especially stimulating work; among students of his imagery one must mention in particular Alexander Holder-Barell and Robert L. Gale; and a host of other critics have provided insights that I was to assimilate in enlarging my sense of what James was doing in his art. One cannot hope to list them all.

I wish to thank Charles Fish of Windham College, who read my first draft, that "loose and baggy monster," and provided innumerable helpful comments. Robert L. Gale's extraordinarily meticulous and wise commentary on the manuscript proved invaluable. I am grateful to Bertram Sarason, editor of *The Connecticut Review*, both for his warm encouragement and for permission to quote from my articles, "The Theme of Freedom in James's *The Tragic Muse*" and " 'The Full Ironic Truth' in *The Spoils of Poynton*." I thank also the editors of *PMLA* and of *Criticism* for permission to quote portions of my articles "The Divided Self in the Fiction of Henry James" and "The Ironic Imagery and Symbolism of James's *The Ambassadors*."

The Crystal Cage

We were all so fine and formal, and the ladies in particular at once so little and so much clothed, so beflounced yet so denuded, that the summer stars called to us in vain. We had ignored them in our crystal cage, among our tinkling lamps; no more free really to alight than if we had been dashing in a locked railway-train across a lovely land.

The Sacred Fount

Introduction

In 1907, after Henry James had submitted his one-act play *The Saloon* to the Incorporated Stage Society, Bernard Shaw (who had found the play so pessimistic that he felt it would tend to "break men's spirits") wrote to James asking: "Why have you done this? . . . Why do you preach cowardice to an army which has victory always and easily within its reach?"[1] James replied:

> I do such things because I happen to be a man of imagination and taste, extremely interested in life, and because the imagination thus, from the moment direction and motive play upon it from all sides, absolutely enjoys and insists on and incurably leads a life of its own, for which just this vivacity itself is its warrant. . . . Half the beautiful things that the benefactors of the human species have produced would surely be wiped out if you don't allow this adventurous and speculative imagination its rights.[2]

The play of "this adventurous and speculative imagination," which "incurably leads a life of its own," is the subject of this book—a subject of the highest importance, I believe, not only to the literary critic but also to the general student of art and culture. For while we are accustomed nowadays to acknowledge that the artist's imagination is synthetic or, as Coleridge said, "esemplastic" and accustomed to regard artistic works as self-reflexive, centripetal, and autonomous, what is frequently not appreciated in the study of literary art is the extent to which a highly generalizing imagination like James's reaches out in its effort to synthesize and unify its materials and to convert "natural fact" into "spiritual fact." And if we recognize in particular works the imagination's power to inform everything with its unified vision, too often we fail to appreciate the extent to which many artists' works, taken together, may constitute a single poem—what Wallace Stevens calls "a poem within, and above, a poem."

Now James's imagination was always imperialistic, always reaching out to bring more and more territory under its unified rule. In the work of such a highly generalizing artist, each new book becomes both a continuation and an extension of the early conquests; there are no interruptions in this continuous advance outward from the center. Or, to shift the metaphor, we may say that each new work proliferates from its predecessors. The imagination "incurably leads a life of its own," and once the process of generation has commenced, growth may proceed in a thousand strange and unpredicted ways; yet everything proceeds from the central vision, the generative source. It is this process of proliferation, these adventures of the imagination from its vital center, that constitute the theme of this book.

But why another book on Henry James? And why a book that stresses, as this one does, James's imagery and symbolism—a subject widely examined by critics for more than three decades? The answer is that this study, unlike the many valuable works that have preceded it, stresses the unity of James's imagery, its derviation from a single imaginative center and a consolidated sense of life. I am concerned with an organized and coherent system of images, epithets, and symbols that articulate a single vision in James's novels. James's story "The Figure in the Carpet" may or may not contain his advice on how we ought to read James, but criticism can scarcely ignore a hint as provocative, as fruitful, as that dropped by the artist Vereker, who suggests that "the order, the form, and the texture" of a writer's books may be revealed to the critic if only he can discover amid the apparent maze of plots, characters, and diction the informing "idea":

> Isn't there for every writer [Vereker asks] a particular thing of that sort, the thing that most makes him apply himself, the thing without the effort to achieve which he wouldn't write at all, the very passion of his passion, the part of his business in which, for him, the flame of art burns most intensely? . . . there's an idea in my work without which I wouldn't have given a straw for the whole job. It's the finest fullest intention of the lot, and the application of it has been, I think, a triumph of patience, of ingenuity. I ought to leave that to somebody else to say; but that nobody does say it is precisely what we're talking about. It stretches, this little trick of mine, from book to book, and everything else, compara-

tively, plays over the surface of it. The order, the form, the texture
of my books will perhaps some day constitute for the initiated a
complete representation of it. So it's naturally the thing for the
critic to look for. It strikes me . . . even as the thing for the critic
to find.³

So central is it, James suggests, that once this underlying principle
is found, it accounts for everything in the writer's art:

> My whole lucid effort [says Vereker] gives [the critic] the clue—
> every page and line and letter. The thing's as concrete there as a
> bird in a cage, a bait on a hook, a piece of cheese in a mousetrap.
> It's stuck into every volume as your foot is stuck into your shoe. It
> governs every line, it chooses every word, it dots every i, it places
> every comma. ["The Figure," 15:233]

If Vereker's remarks hold for James's fiction—if there is a dis-
cernible figure in the carpet of James's books—criticism should
be able to show how that central idea "governs every line,"
"chooses every word," "dots every i," and "places every comma."
And that is precisely what I have tried to do in this study. Taking
Vereker's hint, I have tried to view James's work "closely" and
"analytically" as the expression of "the very passion of his passion," the articulation of his "finest fullest intention," and to
exhibit "the order, the form, the texture" of his novels as the
inevitable consequence of that central vision.

The existence of a figure in the carpet of James's fiction has
been disputed for many years by critics; and those who have
sought to define that figure have often disagreed sharply as to
what it is. Yet these disagreements have arisen chiefly, I think,
because critics have simply been emphasizing different aspects of
James's art—and because they have often neglected the sort of
formalist criticism that Northrop Frye has recommended: the
study of meaning as it is disclosed in the structure of the writer's
images. Now, however, at a time when criticism has gradually
sifted out a number of mistaken views about James the man and
when narrow perspectives on James's art have gradually widened,
it has become clear to most perceptive students of the fiction that
whatever the ostensible subjects of the texts, in book after book
the central concern remains the threat to the "free spirit" who
would "live"—live his own life, unhampered by the people,

institutions, and conventions that always threaten personal freedom. As early as 1918, Ezra Pound identified this passion of James's passion:

> What I have not heard is any word of the major James, of the hater of tyranny; book after early book against oppression, against all the sordid petty personal crushing oppression, the domination of modern life, not worked out in the diagrams of Greek tragedy, not labeled "epos" or "Aeschylus." The outbursts in *The Tragic Muse,* the whole of "The Turn of the Screw," human liberty, personal liberty, the rights of the individual against all sorts of intangible bondage! The passion of it, the continual passion of it in this man who, fools said, didn't "feel."[4]

And since Pound's outburst, a number of critics—of whom the most notable perhaps is Quentin Anderson—have discerned, in various ways, the importance of the ideas of "living" and "freedom" in James's art. The convergent evidence to support the claim that the figure in the carpet is a figure of freedom and enslavement is indeed overwhelming, and I shall present here a great deal of fresh evidence in support of it. For the present, I would only point out parenthetically that James himself supplies a clue to his central concern in the very story in which critics are advised to search out the figure. If we return to Vereker's reply to the critic who has vainly sought the "secret" of Vereker's work, we can scarcely fail to observe that Vereker has in fact provided the clue: "The thing's as concrete there as a bird in a cage, a bait on a hook, a piece of cheese in a mouse-trap." Why these particular images? Vereker would seem to be teasing the critic. But since the critic has asked Vereker for a clue to the figure, it is also possible that the artist is obliging the poor man, knowing perfectly well that the critic will be too unimaginative in any event to pick up the clue. A bird in a cage, a bait on a hook, a piece of cheese in a mousetrap: are these clues to Vereker's work? But even if they were, the reader could never know because James doesn't interpret Vereker's work or supply any substantial information about it.

So the suspicion emerges that in this curious passage James is indulging what Robert Frost calls the pleasure of "ulteriority." At a time when his novels were not being read and when his *Guy Domville* had received the exquisite criticism of hoots and jeers

and roars "like those of a cage of beasts at some infernal 'zoo,' "
it is plausible that James might have wished to drop some clue to
his intention. In his exasperation over the neglect he had suffered
and over the failure of even intelligent readers to understand
what he was about, he might well have felt that he would tell
them what he was about, not in a Shavian preface, but in a stroke
so delicate that they would be certain to miss that too! If they
missed the figure in the carpet, they would certainly miss the
clue to the figure. What was there, after all, that they didn't, in
their benumbed and besotted insensibility, miss?

James's novels examine with indefatigable persistence the
cages, hooks, and traps employed by the enslaving world; they
look into the subtlest means of denying the possibilities of the
free spirit. The novels explore enslavement as systematically as
Dante explores hell—both slavery imposed from without and
inner slavery, the bondage to passion and psychic necessities. And
all of the subsidiary themes of James's work—above all, the "international theme"—may most fruitfully be viewed in relation to
this central idea. For whatever else they may be in the fiction,
"Europe" and "America" are synonyms for enslavement. America
is the cage of "the sacred rage"—of a Puritanism, an "earnestness," a propriety so intense that it denies all wholesome sensuous
knowledge, all delight in artifice and in "the vain appearance."
America is the trap of business, of a relentless determination to
bully and dominate through practical acumen; it is the hook of
a way of life so self-centered, so impervious to foreign influences,
that it prejudges and foredooms whatever is different from itself
as corrupt, monstrous, unnatural. "Europe," on the other hand,
is the cage of the past, of history, of a stamped-out, arranged life
dominated by a rigid tradition, by the Catholic Church, by feudalism, and by standards of conduct imposed by the unchanging
dead. It is the trap of bright appearances, of "things," *objets
d'art,* "collections," of a materialism that ironically is taken to be
the spirit's highest refinement and that masquerades as "culture"
and "civilization." It is the hook of invidious display and show,
invidious manners and proprieties. Neither "America" nor
"Europe" permits its puppets to live and breathe; they demand,
these imperious opposites, only conformity, obedience, "surrender." The man who won't submit—the large-minded spirit

who remains detached, unable to join one party or choose between ugly alternatives—may lose the practical battle of life. "Variety of imagination," James asks, "what is that but fatal in the world of affairs unless so disciplined as not to be distinguished from monotony?" (*Golden Bowl,* 23:128). The refusal to be single-minded constitutes a terrible loss of effectiveness, and those who operate on the world's premises prove fittest in the struggle for survival. It is only in the effort to escape the world's trap that James's free spirits triumph—in their own fashion. They may be heroic; they may be pathetic; but at least they are not birds in a cage, hooked fish, broken-backed mice in the world's, in life's, great trap.

Now the effort to view the whole of James's work closely and analytically as an expression of his "finest fullest intention" can significantly enlarge our sense of what James is doing in his art. For to trace the pattern "from book to book" as it grows and spreads itself out in a hundred rich and surprising exfoliations— to see the beginnings of the pattern in *Roderick Hudson* and *The American,* to follow its luxuriant development in *The Portrait of a Lady* and in the novels of the eighties, to trace its branchings and unexpected turns in the experimental novels of the nineties, and then to behold its extraordinary completions in his last novels—is to realize that the vision required a lifetime of patience and ingenuity for its creation. One realizes, too, that in perfecting his art James sought to make every word and phrase articulate and extend the symbolic scheme whose development was inseparable from the figure in the carpet. By the time he wrote *The Wings of the Dove* James had developed his symbolism so richly that there was no part of human experience he could not incorporate into his design. The vocabulary of "correspondences" was by 1903 virtually complete, and James could find the symbolic equivalents of anything under the sun— or over it. And as one of the chief insights provided by our approach, we can see why his later style had to become mannered, odd, difficult. Critics account for this stylistic complexity by noting that the determination to create a psychological novel, a novel of intense subjectivity, necessitated certain stylistic convolutions. But there was, as well, another principle at work in the production of that magnificent (if sometimes maddening) style: the effort to make everything symbolic, to convert undigested natural fact into symbolic fact, to create a world of perfectly integrated correspondences. James, no less than Dante, was determined to discover the moral significance of every part of human experience. "Convert! convert!" James's father used to admonish his children; and James was determined to convert the waste and dross of life into experience thoroughly evaluated and thoroughly understood, experience whose significance was defined in every sentence by the rich and flexible symbolism that issued from his vision of freedom and entrapment.

To speak of the idea of freedom and entrapment as informing the whole of James's work may, however, be misleading. Critics are sometimes tempted to read literary works as the mere expressions of ideas or philosophies, so reducing complex aesthetic wholes to inflexible intellectual structures. This procedure is, indeed, a fault of one of the most interesting studies of James written in the past two decades, Quentin Anderson's *The American Henry James*. But the truth is that ideas are only a part of the artist's vision; and if we would describe the entire process of James's art we cannot overlook his unique sense of life, the temperamental and moral economy that stands behind his selection of a subject, his evaluation of his characters, and his structuring of images and plots.

James, as we know, saw himself as one of those who take life indirectly. His detachment was "foreseen and foredoomed"; he was preoccupied with his inability to take an active role in the affairs of the world. Condemned to "the madness of art," he saw his whole life in much the same way as he saw Zola's: as Zola existed to write the Rougon-Macquart novels, James existed to create the human comedy of Anglo-American experience. He was incurably a "monster of *Dis*sociation and Detachment," forever the observer, the recorder, the man of imagination, condemned to loneliness and his religion of art. Other, more worldly beings pursued their objectives without wavering or compromise or loss of energy. In his own way James was quite as determined and aggressive as these *hommes du monde*; but unlike them, he was condemned to "variety of imagination," all but fatal in the world of affairs. Others were fixed on "success"; James, while he too wanted success, remained fixed on the development of his imagination.

Thus he was "free" because he was disinterested, because he had no ax to grind, no personal interest in the outcome of his speculations. Like his Gabriel Nash, James had no desire to force others into his boat or to bully them into helping him row it. He was free because he refused to play the world's game: his taking of life "indirectly," his passive observation, and his passion for looking instead of acting were all bound up with his freedom. As for the active ones of the earth, they lived to do the world's work for the world's base purposes;[5] their exertions for personal advantage, their incessant struggles for power and money and "success"—these efforts constituted their enslavement.

So James's ideas are inseparable from his temperamental response to life. The idea of freedom is bound up with a retreat from "active" life, a disinclination for the "ferocity" of competition, a "foreseen and foredoomed detachment." And his fiction, from beginning to end, becomes concerned inevitably with the predicament of the "free spirit"—that is, a divided and relatively passive individual—in a world of enslaving—consolidated and active—aggressors.

It is this "idioverse"—defined by Saul Rosenzweig as "a universe of events . . . with its own inherent structure and trends"—that I explore in the first chapter of this study. My approach may suggest the method of "idiodynamics" which Rosenzweig used in his essay "The Ghost of Henry James," but there is a crucial difference between that psychoanalytic approach and the approach employed here. Instead of using the fiction to interpret the author, to unearth his buried fears and desires, I have used the author's "sense of life" as an aid (and only as an aid) in interpreting the fiction. I have no desire to use the fiction for purposes of psychoanalyzing James. Indeed, psychoanalytic readings of his fiction seem to me, in many instances, distressingly reductive and simplistic. In concentrating on the author's buried fears and desires, such readings tend to ignore the truth that the imagination "incurably leads a life of its own" and to do violence to the fiction considered as fiction. Character, action, and imagery become strategies of a beleaguered psyche trying to "express" unconscious motives, while the artistic requirements of the fiction are often simply ignored. The artist's freedom as a purposive intelligence and as a man of imagination, together with the impersonal character of his art, frequently is either ignored or denied, leaving the reader with a picture of a blind psychic mechanism, a pathetically helpless author condemned to the ingenuous expression of latent anxieties or wishes.

If we would understand the work of art as art, however, we are bound to respect its premises and to heed its inner logic. The formal character of the work must be our starting point. We must ask how the work is structured on its own terms: what it requires, as an artistic whole, to constitute a persuasive image of life. Once we have determined the principle of unity in the artistic whole, we are in a position to proceed further: to see the story not merely on its own terms, but as a reflection of a total "sense of life"; and if we are acute, we may then come to see a figure extending from line to line and story to story, a figure constituting a single vision of which all the author's works are the representation. The focus of such a criticism is not, however, the author's life. Although the bearing of James's life on his fiction is often illuminating and I shall frequently have occasion to point out connections between his personal anxieties and the conflicts dramatized in his fiction, my essential concern is the habits of his imagination. My aim is to show how this imagination selects and shapes its materials over an entire lifetime and how, in its adventures, it seeks to extend and complicate the figure in the carpet.

In the first chapter, then, I try to show how James's sense of life fuses with his "ideas" to create the unique perspective that informs all of his fiction. Thereafter, I have sought to show how this vision realizes itself in the most significant elements of his art: in characterization, action, and imagery.

In his characterization, James creates two great camps of "active" aggressors—those attached to the "old" and those attached to the "new"—and he places between them a "free spirit," drawn toward both camps but resisting both, a "divided self," unwilling (or unable) to take sides, to join one camp or the other. The extent to which this divided self is, in book after book, the center of James's art has not been fully appreciated by critics; yet many of the debates over the nature of his heroes and heroines— particularly Isabel Archer, Nick Dormer, Nanda Brookenham, and Fleda Vetch—can be resolved once we grasp this fundamental principle at work in James's creation and alignment of characters. The action of James's fiction dramatizes the struggles of the "free spirit" as he encounters, evades, resists, escapes from, or succumbs to one form of entrapment after another. As James steadily complicates his vision of "the great trap of life," so I trace the gradual extension of the figure in the carpet. We witness the young James's attack on the tyranny of convention and propriety in the early fiction; then his consideration of political and social movements—socialism, conservatism, the suffragette movement, male authoritarianism—that seek to "get hold of" the free spirit in the novels of the eighties; his analysis of the trap of the career in *The Tragic Muse;* and finally James's cold picture of the acquisitive world of power, money, and conspicuous display in the novels of the nineties and of his major phase—a picture darkened by his renderings of the slavery that arises from within, from need and desire and fear.

In dealing with James's imagery and symbolism, I describe the major clusters that arise inevitably not only from James's desire to dramatize the plight of the free spirit but also from his tendency to express the tensions within his own personality. James's "imagination of disaster" is most fully articulated in three major groups: the images and symbols of warfare and aggression; of the enslaving world of the eye, appearances, and acting; and of the cage, immobility, petrifaction and passivity.

Finally, I turn to James's criticism, for it too is bound up with the idea of freedom. His criticism and fiction are inseparable, reflecting a unified sense of life and a recurrent condemnation of narrowness, partiality, and prejudice. In his criticism, then, as in his fiction, the key terms are "life"and "freedom." Although some critics, such as Wayne C. Booth, Robert Scholes, and Robert Kellogg, have argued that James was defending a very limited version of realism, James's premises and his reasonings remain precious for those concerned, as James was, with mimetic fidelity —the creation of the most persuasive and authentic image of life.

A few words on the way in which this study grew and acquired its present shape may help the reader to understand the critical approach. The book originated in a number of studies of particular novels and tales—in my efforts as a formalist critic to determine the shaping principle of each story and the expression of that principle in all parts of James's work. I then set about bringing together the insights that existed in a dozen separate studies and in my notes on James. My approach, in short, was inductive, though the form of presentation in this book may at times suggest a deductive method. The point is that the figure in the carpet was discovered in the fiction; it was not imposed.

I hasten to add, however, that I have no intention of reducing James's work to the figure in the carpet or of claiming that the figure is *the* key to James's work. Art is always richer than our critical analyses, and the "meaning" of James's art, like that of Shakespeare's or Melville's, is inexhaustible. Particularly in tracing out the structure of James's images and symbols, I may seem to ignore elements in the fiction that might well be considered if one is to arrive at a rich and rounded interpretation of each work. For example, I have not recorded that the images of chains and cages in *The Ambassadors* are in some contexts clearly comic; that the figure of the "bulging eyes" of the Catholic Church is *Waymarsh*'s image and is comically biased, certainly not part of Strether's unfolding understanding of Europe; that it is absurd to imagine the indefatigable, self-righteous Sarah Pocock as really being "bricked up" or "buried alive"; and so on. Yet even in comic or cheerful contexts James employs a vocabulary that everywhere articulates his central vision of life. And to justify any omission of references to James's comic sense (admirably dealt with by such critics as Richard Poirier and Ian Watt), I would only say—as I do at the end of Chapter 3—that I have sought to stress here what James calls "the *full* ironic truth" of his fiction. If we would understand James's vision—and the nature of his images of life—it is this truth that must be emphasized.

James is so preoccupied with the articulation of his ironic vision that a great many terms which ordinarily would be read as having no symbolic implications whatever absorb, by virtue of their participation in an organic pattern extending throughout the work, meanings derived from the pattern as a whole. Consider the vocabulary of profit, gain, loss, owing, etc. in *The Spoils of Poynton*. In daily intercourse we often use this vocabulary without any awareness of its commercial implications. We hope

to "gain" or "profit" from a book or a lecture; we "owe" our
thanks or our respect to another person; we suffer a "loss" of
prestige, etc. The metaphors are dead and we intend that they
should remain dead. But when the subject of a novel is the
"spoils," the "things," the struggle for possession of objects
having rare value; when even the heroine is revealed as having a
desire to preside as queen mother over Poynton; when, in short,
the basic conflict of the action is concerned with material gains or
losses, then the dead metaphors suddenly come alive. Fleda's
"commerce" with Mrs. Gereth becomes far more than social intercourse or discussion. A conceptual substitution occurs: such
"commerce" is indeed a form of commercial avidity—it refers to
actions tainted by economic motives. In the context no innocent
reading of the word *commerce* is possible. Fleda's motives are
only apparently pure.

Generally speaking, words acquire symbolic meaning in
literary works when they are placed in antithetical patterns.
(Blake's "tiger" is defined sharply by his "lamb.") Symbolism
derives from basic conflict: the ideal is opposed to the material,
light to dark, freedom to slavery, renunciation to hedonism, and
so on. Moreover, as I have pointed out in *Symbolism: The Manichean Vision*,[6] the symbol gathers meaning by absorbing into itself all of the relevant associates of the entire pattern of which
it is a part. What is "relevant" to the word *commerce* in *The
Spoils of Poynton* is the entire pattern of financial and commercial
terms used to describe the actions of James's characters. And this
pattern is developed in ironic conjunction with the vocabulary
of religion, idealism, and spiritual loftiness. (James himself calls
attention to the ironic oppositions of his images and symbols
when he speaks in the Preface to *The Spoils* of an appetite
that brings to mind "brazen idols and precious metals and inserted gems in the tempered light of some arching place of worship" [10:xii].) And because James worked typically with such
antithetical patterns, it is frequently the case that a term taken at
first blush to be an image[7] is really a symbol—that is, a form of
conceptual, not merely of verbal, substitution.[8] When Strether
says to Chad that the latter would be "a brute" if he deserted
Madame de Vionnet, the critic must decide: Does Strether mean
that Chad would be acting barbarously ("brute" as a dead meta-

phor for barbarous behavior)? Does he mean that Chad would be acting like a brute (thus verbal substitution, an image)? Or does he mean that in some sense Chad would actually be a brute, that is a lower animal, a beast? The extensive animal imagery in *The Ambassadors*—imagery used to designate the predatory nature of the social animals in the circus-ring of the world and designed to underscore the paradox that this apparently refined civilization is really a jungle—compels us to regard "brute" not merely as a dead metaphor or as an image but as a symbol. The "full ironic truth" of this passage is that Chad is scarcely "human." The appetites of the brute dictate all of his conduct, and he is part of the jungle that lies behind the fair appearance of a civilized world. In James's most mature work, the appearance is almost never the reality. In this reading of James the stress on the antithetical patterns of his symbolism[9] is necessary if we would deal with his vocabulary in terms of the basic conflicts which it seeks to dramatize with maximum expressiveness.

I have said that in examining James's imagery and symbolism I try to show which categories are major and why, given James's vision of life, they had to be major. By a major category I mean one that generates and subsumes lesser categories; it is a category having such generality and such power of implication that it continually nourishes and guides the imagination in its search for the *mot juste*. The antitheses of art and nature, of aggression and passivity, of freedom and enslavement, are central because they breed enormous families of more limited scope and power of implication. They breed, for example, many of James's water images which stress the idea of passivity—of being swept along by a current or allowing oneself to float, thus surrendering to conditions or to traditions (in contrast to active exertion for the sake of freedom). This motif is particularly prominent in *The Wings of the Dove*, but the association of water imagery and passivity is recurrent throughout James's work (as Robert L. Gale has demonstrated),[10] and it is the idea of passivity that dictates the use of water imagery. Again, much of the extensive imagery of religion in James's work in connected with the idea of enslavement or surrender to an enslaving dogma or tradition. Robert Gale points out, "Jamesian people are likened to functionaries and communicants of the Catholic church, from priests and confessors, and nuns and monks, to devout pilgrims and persons cherishing rosary, medal and cross."[11] Many of these functionaries have surrendered their freedom and are enslaved by their vows of obedience: like Morris Gedge of "The Birthplace," who becomes "the priest of the idol" when he becomes curator of the supposed birthplace of Shakespeare and is forced to take orders from Mr. Grant-Jackson, the man who is like "a beast-tamer in a cage"; like Hyacinth Robinson of *The Princess Casamassima,* who takes "a vow of blind obedience, the vow as of the Jesuit fathers to the head of their order" (6:54); like Pansy Osmond or Jeanne de Vionnet, passive votaries and stereotypes; or Miriam Rooth of *The Tragic Muse,* surrendering herself utterly to her career as an actress and becoming "the priestess on the tripod, awaiting the afflatus and thinking only of that" (7:126); or Milly Theale, imprisoned by her wealth and by the crystal cage of society, with her "infinite number of yards of priceless lace" hanging "down to her feet like the stole of a priestess" (*Wings,* 20:96); or Fleda Vetch, worshipping at the "shrine" of Poynton; or Lambert Strether, surrendering for a time to "Europe," his hands "embrued with the blood of monstrous alien altars—of another faith altogether" (*The Ambassadors,* 22:167–68); and so on. A very long list of the religious images connected with enslavement might be compiled (there are many excellent examples in Gale's *The Caught Image,* pp. 148–66). It goes without saying, however, that religious imagery may also be employed for other purposes; one is to dramatize the effort of a free spirit to rise above an enslaving pagan world, as when Maggie Verver becomes symbolically the sacrificial lamb and the redeemer.

Several other abundant clusters of images might be mentioned in this connection—for example, imagery of heights and depressions, of old age and youth, of the West and the East—but I have passed over these (and many others) not only because I wish to avoid repetition but also because they can be derived easily, I believe, from James's major, generative categories. My focus is on categories indisputably central in James's imagination, and I have traced in detail James's handling of these central images and symbols (and of many of their associates) from book to book over his career. The figure in the carpet emerges sharply from this analysis of the structure of his images; and the subtlety—the

thoroughly organic nature—of James's imagery, its perfect in-
evitability, are here displayed to demonstrate that "everything
else, comparatively, plays over the surface" of James's art.

1
James's Sense of Life

If, as Willa Cather once remarked, all of a writer's most valuable material is acquired before he reaches the age of fifteen, Henry James's *A Small Boy and Others* might be expected to contain the richest material available both for shedding light on the personal problems with which James was concerned when he composed his fiction and for illuminating our understanding of the basic themes of his work. When we find, moreover, that his memoir tends to sound, in the most disparate contexts, a single note and to sound it emphatically, we may feel sure that our examination of the reverberations of that note is bound to yield immense insight into the manifest and latent content of his work. The note that hums most persistently through the pages of *A Small Boy and Others* is one of envy; and it is so far from being an unconscious motif of the memoir that James felt it necessary to devote two pages to an explicit analysis of his state of mind.

> . . . I may remark here that though in that early time I seem to have been constantly eager to exchange my lot for that of somebody else, on the assumed certainty of gaining by the bargain, I fail to remember feeling jealous of such happier persons—in the measure open to children of spirit. I had rather a positive lack of the passion, and thereby, I suppose, a lack of spirit; since if jealousy bears, as I think, on what one sees one's companions able to do— as against one's own falling short—envy, as I knew it at least, was simply of what they *were,* or in other words of a certain sort of richer consciousness supposed, doubtless often too freely supposed, in them. They were so *other*—that was what I felt; and to *be* other, other almost anyhow, seemed as good as the probable taste of the bright compound wistfully watched in the confectioner's window; unattainable, impossible, of course, but as to which just this impossibility and just that privation kept those active proceedings in which jealously seeks relief quite out of the question. A

platitude of acceptance of the poor actual, the absence of all vision
of how in any degree to change it, combined with a complacency,
an acuity of perception of alternatives, though a view of them as
only through the confectioner's hard glass—that is what I recover
as the nearest approach to an apology, in the soil of my nature, for
the springing seed of emulation. I never dreamed of competing—
a business having in it at the best, for my temper, if not for my
total failure of temper, a displeasing ferocity. If competing was
bad snatching was therefore still worse, and jealousy was a sort
of spiritual snatching. With which, nevertheless, all the while, one
might have been "like" So-and-So, who had such horizons. A helpless little love of horizons I certainly cherished, and could sometimes
even care for my own. These always shrank, however, under almost
any suggestion of a further range or finer shade in the purple rim
offered to other eyes—and that is what I take for the restlessness of
envy. It wasn't that I wished to change with everyone, with anyone
at a venture, but that I saw "gifts" everywhere but as mine and that
I scarce know whether to call the effect of this miserable or monstrous. It was the effect at least of self-abandoment—I mean to
visions.[1]

He was not jealous because there was simply no question of
competing with others. Yet "the restlessness of envy," with its
attendant effect of the "miserable" or the "monstrous," he regards
as an apparently ineradicable affliction of his nature. If, however,
envy was so intensely a preoccupation of his consciousness, we can
surely learn much if we ask why it was so important for him to
be "other" and then what the effect on his writing was of his
apparently incorrigible yearning.

The answer to the first question is to be found everywhere in
the pages of *A Small Boy and Others*. The inferiority complex is
as common as grass, and there is no question that James was its
victim.[2] Nor was it the simple outgrowth of his sense that he
was hopelessly behind his brother William, that he could not
possibly catch up. That is a part of the story, and by no means
(as Leon Edel has shown) the least significant part; but what is
equally plain, for James as well as for the reader of his memoir,
is that he felt himself temperamentally debarred from "life," from
action, from "going in" for things, from the "displeasing ferocity"

of competition. There was, he tells us—in a phrase so pertinent to his case that he repeats it twice (pp. 213, 226): his "foreseen and foredoomed detachment"—his temperamental incapacity to give himself to anything, any cause, any person. Always he was to be the onlooker, "taking in" but, unlike his brother Wilky, incapable of "going in" for things and people:

> There was the difference and the opposition, as I really believe I was already aware—that one way of taking life was to go in for everything and everyone, which kept you abundantly occupied, and the other way was to be as occupied, quite as occupied, just with the sense and the image of it all, and on only a fifth of the actual immersion: a circumstance extremely strange. Life was taken almost equally both ways—that, I mean, seemed the strangeness; mere brute quantity and number being so much less in one case than the other. These latter were what I should have liked to go in for, had I but had the intrinsic faculties. . . . [*Small Boy*, p. 290]

His sense of his incapacity to live life directly and passionately is so intense that almost any reference to "brute quantity and number"—almost any reference, that is, to the practical mastery of life, to business acumen, to military prowess, to adventure, to action and competence—arouses his envy. If he himself has a "comparatively so indirect faculty for what is called taking life" (p. 288), if he is cut off from "direct participation" (p. 194), Wilky takes it with an astonishing directness; and his cousins' "mere reality of relation" and "commoner directness of contact" make them loom as "divinities or demons" (p. 195). If Henry "never dreamed of competing," if his competitions were "with nobody, or nobody's with me," his brother William's competitions were "with others—in which how wasn't he, how could he not be, successful?" (pp. 207-8). William plays with "boys who curse and swear!" (p. 259). If Henry's case is "intrinsically of the poorest," if he shows "rare inaptitudes" (p. 193) or an "aptitude showing for nil" (p. 325), others know how, others have mastered life:

> Nothing in truth is more distinct to me than the tune to which they [his schoolmates] were, without exception, at their ease on such a ground—unless it be my general dazzled, humiliated sense, through those years, of the common, the baffling, mastery, all round me, of a hundred handy arts and devices. Everyone did things and had things—everyone knew how, even when it was a question of

the small animals, the dormice and grasshoppers, or the hoards of food and stationery, that they kept in their desks, just as they kept in their heads such secrets for how to do sums—those secrets that I must even then have foreseen I should even so late in life as this have failed to discover. [*Small Boy*, p. 223]

If he is given to seeking "substitutes for lost causes," others seize their opportunities and act (p. 302). The slightest encounter with action, whether mastery, power, aggressiveness, or directness, evokes his admiration and wonder. There is cousin Albert, for example, who "had in a remote part of the State a vast wild property of his own, known as the Beaverkill, to which . . . he vainly invited W. J. and me. . . . the place was in the wilderness, incalculably distant, reached by a whole day's rough drive from the railroad, through every danger of flood and field, with prowling bears thrown in and probable loss of limb, of which there were sad examples, from swinging scythes and axes; but we of course measured our privation just by those facts, and grew up . . . to believe that pleasures beyond price had been cruelly denied us" (pp. 124–25). With his "air of possibilities" Cousin Albert suggests to the young James such "a wild freedom" as the poor introvert can never know (p. 121). Then there is the "boy called Simpson," who "reeked, to my sense, with strange acomplishment —no single show of which but was accompanied in him by a smart protrusion of the lower lip, a crude complacency of power, that almost crushed me to sadness" (pp. 224–25). There are the Ward brothers, whose rusticity "hadn't prevented the annexation of whole tracts of town life unexplored by ourselves and achieved by the brothers since their relatively recent migration from Connecticut" (p. 245)—while James, even on a night of revelry, felt that he couldn't "indeed have moved much . . . I must have kept intensely still in my corner, all wondering and all fearing—fearing notice most. . . . Mrs. L. and I must have been the only persons not shaking a foot. . . ." (pp. 43–44). There are the boys at school: "It wasn't that the boys swarming for us at school were not often, to my vision, unlimited, but that those peopling our hours of ease, as I have already noted, were almost inveterately so—they seemed to describe always, out of view, so much larger circles" (pp. 257–58). And there are the "Fezandié young men" who "were as much abroad as might be" and who appeared on the

Champs-Elysées while James was "walking sedately either with my mother or my aunt"; "armed for conquest, or at the least for adventure," one of them greeted James and his mother "with a grace that was as a beat of the very wings of freedom!" (pp. 376–78.)

In all these passages and in many more, James portrays himself as a creature so temperamentally estranged from the practical business of living that, like Lambert Strether, he is not only not at home in the world—he is made a fool of by it. Nothing glows for him so brightly as adventure, glamor, conquest, the theatrical, the wild, the free; but there is nothing he is less capable of "going in for": such is the curse of his "foreseen and foredoomed detachment."

But James does not blame temperament exclusively. If he feels that others do and have, while he cannot, he traces at least part of this incapacity to his parents—and especially to his father. I am not referring to Oedipal problems or anything similar (which I leave to the psychiatrists), but simply to one very obvious fact that caused James anxiety in his youth: the fact that, as all the children seem to have felt, the family was disconnected from any solid, established world, the fact that it was nomadic, impossible to classify. Bad enough that James was himself temperamentally detached from life; but when his family was also detached, when the only air he could breathe from the first was that of a vague, inward nonattachment, he must have felt that there was simply no chance for him to do what a part of him so deeply craved: to establish himself in the world, to participate in life. "Live!" Strether exhorts Little Bilham, and "living" is the great theme of James's fiction. But lacking "passion" and "spirit," where could he get the help he needed to live directly, to overcome his shyness and "go in" for things, if not from his family? But if they could provide no example of established and resourceful worldliness for him to follow, offering only disconnectedness, where was he except adrift, left to his own resources—resources that he knew perfectly well he did not have?

The note of resentment toward his family is muted in the memoir, yet it is unmistakably there. It sounds clearly in his comments on his father's scheme to let his children freely choose their own church. The consequence of the father's insistence on free choice was that the children, William and Henry, felt they had no identity, and anxiety rose in them whenever they were asked, "What church do you go to?" (p. 233). Their "pewless state," James comments, "involved, to my imagination, much the same discredit that a houseless or a cookless would have done." He continues: "It was colder than any criticism, I recall, to hear our father reply that we could plead nothing less than the whole privilege of Christendom and that there was no communion, even that of the Catholics, even that of the Jews, even that of the Swedenborgians, from which we need find ourselves excluded" (p. 234). But the young James "not only failed quite to rise to the parental reasoning, but made out in it rather a certain sophistry; such a prevarication for instance as if we had habitually said we kept the carriage we observably didn't keep. . . ." (p. 235).

It was important to him apparently—to that envious part of his soul—that he be something, something solid and identifiable.[3] Yet he was not anything that could be defined. It would have counted for something to have a public school education, as the Ward brothers had had ("We must have been in relation with no other feeders at the public trough of learning—I can't account otherwise for the glamour as of envied privilege and strange experience that surrounded the Wards" [*Small Boy*, p. 246]), but instead there had been the succession of private schools and tutors, the wandering, the endless experimentation. It would have been something to be solidly rooted in America, yet from the beginning his "young allegiance" was "split . . . into such unequal halves" by Louis De Coppet, son of a French family that in New York "enjoyed the pre-eminence of being European" (p. 32). The "supersubtle Louis," who invited James to collaborate with him in the writing of a romance, brought home to the young American the "sense of Europe"; "His the toy hammer that drove in the very point of the golden nail" (pp. 34, 35). So James was nailed to division and contradiction, even as Lambert Strether was pierced by the "little golden nail" driven by Madame de Vionnet. Again, it would have been something to be "formed," to acquire social grace and sophistication, but, James writes: "We came more or less to see that our young contemporaries of another world, the trained and admonished, the disciplined and governessed, or in a word the formed, relatively speaking, had been made aware of many things of which those at home hadn't been. . . ." (p. 55).

Even more serious, for the young lad who was to aspire to become another "prodigious Balzac," was his total want of exposure to "life" in the form of business (*Small Boy*, p. 374). For if the business of America was indeed business, then the American Balzac sorely needed knowledge of the counting house. But he had none at all: "Business in a world of business was the thing we most agreed . . . in knowing nothing about" (p. 58). And the consequence of his confinement to the "limited pasture" of the James family—the pasture from which "things of the world" were inevitably excluded—was, for Henry and for the other children, so severe that it constituted an evil almost unmitigated (pp. 190, 191). Speaking of the family's "sudden collective disconnectedness (ours as the whole kinship's) from *the* American resource of those days," James says:

> That precious light was the light of "business" only; and we, by a common instinct, artlessly joining hands, went forth into the wilderness without so much as a twinkling taper.
>
> Our consensus, on all this ground, was amazing—it brooked no exception; the word had been passed, all round, that we didn't, that we couldn't and shouldn't, understand these things, questions of arithmetic and of fond calculation, questions of the counting-house and the market; and we appear to have held to our agreement as loyally and to have accepted our doom as serenely as if our faith had been mutually pledged. The rupture with my grandfather's tradition and attitude was complete; we were never in a single case, I think, for two generations, guilty of a stroke of business; the most that could be said of us was that, though about equally wanting, all round, in any faculty of acquisition, we happened to pay for the amiable weakness less in some connections than in others. The point was that we moved so oddly and consistently— as it was our only form of consistency—over our limited pasture, never straying to nibble in the strange or the steep places. [*Small Boy*, pp. 189–90]

They paid less in some connections than in others, but always they paid. Van Wyck Brooks's comments on James's early sense of deprivation are well taken. For the child who paid most dearly was perhaps the one who wished to be the great master of the realistic novel, whose appointed mission was to represent the world in its truest colors, the man who said of the craft of fiction that not only was it necessary for the writer to take notes, he could never take enough notes. But of the world of business his notebook was barren: Balzac with no knowledge, not a jot, of the money-making art![4]

So the wonderful freedom that Henry James, Sr., was to provide for his children, that freedom to pick and choose and assimilate, and the father's concomitant resistance to their settling upon any definite vocation, was discovered to have one terrible flaw. Freedom to be everything and anything was also freedom to be nothing; and it was the queerness of the James family that they were, in a sense, nothing at all: they were "typeless" (p. 141), "mere earnest nomads" (p. 329). It was characteristic of his father, James remarks in one telling passage, that he "suffered me to dangle"; and in the end the young James was to acquire "a consciousness that was to be nothing if not mixed and a curiosity that was to be nothing if not restless" (pp. 182, 164). Pluralism, relativism, and pragmatism may be good philosophies for some, but for those reared in an atmosphere of typelessness, so powerful is the craving for identity that the absolute, the fixed, the established come to have an almost irresistible appeal. Thus, speaking of his cousin Helen, James says:

> Her value to my imagination is even most of all perhaps in her mere local consistency, her fine old New York ignorance and rigour. Her traditions, scant but stiff, had grown there, close to her—they were all she needed, and she lived by them candidly and stoutly. That there have been persons so little doubtful of duty helps to show us how societies grow. A proportionately small amount of absolute conviction about it will carry, we thus make out, a vast weight of mere comparative. She was as anxious over hers indeed as if it had ever been in question—which is a proof perhaps that being void of imagination, when you are quite entirely void, makes scarcely more for comfort than having too much, which only makes in a manner for a homeless freedom or even at the worst for a questioned veracity. With a big installed conscience there is virtue in a grain of the figurative faculty—it acts as oil to the stiff machine. [*Small Boy,* pp. 122–23]

However dangerous traditions and "consistency" may seem to the experimentalist, pragmatist, or pluralist, they are in a sense preferable to a "homeless freedom" and to the sort of endless shifting of positions that produces "at the worst . . . a questioned veracity." It may be, as the title of a poem by Wallace Stevens has it, that "The Good Man Has No Shape"; but is the shapeless, typeless man authentic? Or is he mere slipperiness and hopeless inconsistency—not solidly a man at all but an endless flux, a nomad, a mere observer of the scene? The small boy, whatever else he was, was certainly "queer," "odd," "strange"—characterizations that recur throughout the memoir (e.g., pp. 131, 190, 88); and his temperamental strangeness was reinforced by the strangeness of his family's way of life. In the end this small boy with the acute sense of possibilities—the boy who, like Hyacinth Robinson, the hero of *The Princess Casamassima*, was born divided and for whom consistency and unity of being acquired a prodigious value—had to settle for himself, for detachment, for inconsistency, for homeless freedom, for a kind of identity in his very lack of identity. He was to appreciate fully the advantages of his lonely cosmopolitan life; but he could not help envying the "placed" and confident condition of those he refers to, in *The Ivory Tower*, as "flagrant worldlings" (25:180).

At this point, however, we might ask whether James's testimony is psychoanalytically valid. It may be argued that the retrospective statements of an elderly man scarcely reveal the actual truth of the childhood experience and that James's "envy," even if frankly acknowledged, is simply an ingredient in what James calls "the history of my fostered imagination." That imagination, the artist's developing consciousness, expands by his assuming that everything not itself is somehow "romantic" and therefore to be desired, to be imaginatively incorporated by the observer into a larger consciousness of life, a richer imagination. To this end, one might point out, James even envies orphans—because their state somehow represents "indefinite possibilities"—but need we conclude that James envies orphans in any literal sense? Now it seems to me that Leon Edel and Saul Rosenzweig have convincingly established the importance of envy both as a psychoanalytic fact of James's early life and as an index to James's later preoccupations. There is evidence in James's letters, too, that clearly points to this conclusion—as I shall show in Chapter 2 in considering the problem of the divided self in James's fiction.

For the present, however, I would point out that the history of James's "fostered imagination" is my chief concern in this study and that no attempt will be made in the pages that follow to reduce his fiction and his categories of thought to a psychic wound. It is sufficient for my purpose to concentrate solely on James's sense of life, on the way in which his imagination characteristically organizes experience. Thus we might adequately account for the passivity-aggression equations in *A Small Boy and Others* by referring not to a psychic insult but to a central fact of James's intellectual life: the climate of opinion in which he grew up inevitably fostered a concern with the problem of enslavement or bullying by worldly aggressors.

Quentin Anderson has demonstrated brilliantly that the ideas of Henry James, Sr., provided the central emphasis of James's thought. The stress on slavery, particularly on the enslaving conditions of society, in the thought of the elder James—the fear of any attachment, any dependence, any fixed and rooted condition of life, the repugnance to "all sickening partisanship," to "educational bigotries," to "the shackles of custom," to fossilized forms and "diseased institutions," together with the hope for a new society in which "innocence shall never be tarnished nor trafficked in, in which man's every freedom shall be respected down to its feeblest filament as the radiant altar of God"—all this, by James's own word, spoke eloquently to him: he "saw that [his] father saw." The family, he says, "felt there was nothing in his [father's] exhibition of life that [his father's ideas] didn't or couldn't account for."[5]

And it would be possible to derive all of James's fiction from a comment such as the following, written by James's father and quoted in *Notes of a Son and Brother*:

> I am sure no man can be put in a position of dependence upon another without that other's very soon becoming—if he accepts the duties of the relation—utterly degraded out of his just human proportions. No man can play the Deity to his fellow man with impunity—I mean spiritual impunity of course. For see: if I am at all satisfied with that relation, if it contents me to be in a position of generosity toward others, I must be remarkably indifferent at bottom to the gross social inequality which permits that position, and instead of resenting the enforced humiliation of my

fellow man to myself, in the interests of humanity, I acquiesce in
it for the sake of the profit it yields to my own self-complacency. . . .
No human being can afford to commit his happiness to another's
keeping, or, what is the same thing, forego his own individuality
with all that it imports. The first requisite of our true relationship
to each other (spiritually speaking) is that we be wholly independent of each other: then we may give ourselves away as much
as we please, we shall do neither them nor ourselves any harm.
[pp. 237, 239]

With ideas like these a part of the very air he breathed in
his youth, ideas reinforced moreover by his temperamental detachment and sense of removal from the aggressive life, it is
small wonder that James began to see signs—or symbols—of enslavement everywhere. Not only was he acutely aware of every
instance of his own "servitude"—of William's dazzling free play
of mind and greater range of experience, of all the instances of
opportunity and action that we have glanced at—he saw enslavement everywhere in his travels.

In 1860, when he was seventeen, for example, there were the
French boys, "with their destiny of ultimate Europeanisation, of
finally complete absorption into the French system, already
rather written for them—as a like history, for like foredoomed
young subjects, was in those years beginning to be prefigured,
through marriages of daughters and other such beguilements,
almost wherever one looked" (*Notes . . . Brother*, p. 18). There
was, when he stayed in Germany at Bonn-am-Rhein, his sense of
confinement: "I recall how oppressively in that apartment, how
congestedly, as in some cage of which the wires had been papered
over, I felt housed and disconnected. . . ." (*Notes . . . Brother*,
p. 30). As for the English, they appeared to him, in 1869, as
"dipped in the crucible, which gives them a sort of coating of
comely varnish and colour. They have been smoothed and
polished by mutual social attrition"; they lack "intellectual grace"
and "moral spontaneity" and they "live wholly in the realm of
the cut and dried" (*Letters*, 1:22, 26). Americans, with "their
perpetual reference of all things to some American standard or
precedent which exists only in their own unscrupulous wind-
bags," fared no better in the opinion of the observant young man
(*Letters*, 1:22). And had he not felt as early as 1867 or '68, on a

journey to Boston with his father—that father whose touch was, James said, "always right" to set in motion the "spring" of his dramatic sense (*Notes* . . . *Brother,* p. 191)—that Boston was a great penitentiary?

> . . . my first impression of Boston gave it to me under certain aspects as more expressive than I had supposed an American city could be of a seated and rooted social order, an order not complex but sensibly fixed—gathered in or folded back to intensity upon itself; and this, again and again, when the compass of the pasture, its narrow field, might almost have made the fold excruciating. [*Notes* . . . *Brother,* p. 190]

There were, moreover, in addition to these cages of race and national origin, the cages of the professions. The "clerical race" he saw already, at seventeen, as "the pre-eminently restrictive tribe"; indeed there was "a civilisation replete with 'ministers'— for we at least knew the word—actively, competitively, indeed as would often appear quite violently, ministering. . . ." (*Notes* . . . *Brother,* p. 170). As for the Pope, when James saw him borne through the streets of Rome in 1869, he was "like some dusky Hindoo idol in the depths of its shrine" (*Letters,* 1:25). But in fact any calling was, by his father's lights, a sort of bondage. William's choices of various scientific subjects were "surrenders" to the cage of science. But so, equally, was Henry's choice of writing:

> When I myself, later on, began to "write" it was breathed upon me with the finest bewildering eloquence, with a power of suggestion in truth which I fairly now count it a gain to have felt play over me, that this too was narrowing. [*Notes* . . . *Brother,* p. 52]

In this connection, the long analysis in *Notes of a Son and Brother* of the influence of John La Farge on James's youth is illuminating. La Farge might have opened doors for young Henry— "prospects and possibilities that made the future flush and swarm" (p. 85)—might have seemed an "agent" far more beneficial than practical men, who were "specialised and stiffened, committed to their one attitude, the immediately profitable" (p. 89). Yet the terms that James uses to describe this artist point unmistakably to the enslavement of art, taste, and aesthetics. La Farge is not liberated from the world but is, precisely, "the man of the world" who reminds James that there is "some larger felt extension roundabout us of 'the world'—a sphere the confines of which move on even as we ourselves move and which is always there, just beyond us, to twit us with the more it should have to show if we were a little more 'of' it" (pp. 89–90). Thus the imagery in a later passage suggests vividly not only the stamped-out product of the world but also a kind of idolatry:

> The wealth of his cultivation, the variety of his initiations, the inveteracy of his forms, the degree of his *empressement* . . . made him, with those elements of the dandy and the cavalier to which he struck us as so picturesquely sacrificing, a cluster of bright promises . . . an embodiment of the gospel of esthetics. [*Notes . . . Brother,* p. 91]

In fact, James was *caged* by this artist: he became, he tells us, the "mere helpless admirer and inhaler, led captive in part by the dawning perception that the arts were after all essentially one and that even with canvas and brush whisked out of my grasp I still needn't feel disinherited" (*Notes . . . Brother,* p. 97). But if he was caged and used (as a model) by the painter, it occurred to him that he too could make La Farge—or at least La Farge's "garden of Mérimée"—serve him: "Didn't I already see, as I fumbled with a pen, of what the small dense formal garden might be inspiringly symbolic?" (p. 98). The garden would suggest, I believe, the art-nature equations that James was to employ so extensively in his fiction and would symbolize the entrapment of spontaneity by art and artifice. Thus Isabel Archer, the spontaneous young woman from Albany, who is "very natural" and whose soul has, as she thinks, "a garden-like quality," would become the portrait, cold, fixed, finished, hung up for conspicuous display in the prison of the Palazzo Roccanera. Thus, too, the garden of the great Gloriani in *The Ambassadors* would become that ambiguous trap in which Strether is caught, the trap in which the revered, the worshipped artist moves like a king crowned with light—moves even with the motion of the world, the confining sphere in which men have so much visual sense that they seem to have no other. For La Farge, like Gloriani, suggests to James a "settled sovereign self" and possesses a serenity which is "capital that must never brook defeat—which it so easily might incur by a single act of abdication" (*Notes . . . Brother,* p. 99). Small wonder that James would speak of his own "acceptances" and "submissions" in regard to art—quite as he spoke of the enslavement to any other profession.

His eye darts everywhere in its search for examples of limitation, of surrenders to a confining way of life. His mother's "smoothness of surrender" to his father and to the family attracts his notice (*Notes . . . Brother,* p. 167). And much as he admired his father's largeness and "selfless detachment" and his "example of living as much as we might in some such light of our own," he sees, even in the grand personal style of that remarkable man, a profound limitation:

> Was not the reason at bottom that I so suffered, I might almost have put it, under the impression of his style, which affected me as somehow too philosophic for life, and at the same time too living, as I made out, for thought?—since I must weirdly have opined that by so much as you were individual, which meant personal, which meant monotonous, which meant limitedly allusive and verbally repetitive, by so much you were not literary or, so to speak, *largely* figurative. My father had terms, evidently strong, but in which I presumed to feel, with a shade of irritation, a certain narrowness of exclusion as to images otherwise—and oh, since it was a question of the pen, so multitudinously!—entertainable. Variety, variety— *that* sweet ideal, *that* straight contradiction of any dialectic, hummed for me all the while as a direct, if perverse and most unedified, effect of the parental concentration, with some of its consequent, though heedless, dissociations. [*Notes . . . Brother,* p. 180]

Life is more various than ideas. And James's recognition that the swarming realities contradict "any dialectic" is the seed of his further recognition that the great mythologies of his age were but so many artfully baited traps set for the uncommitted soul, the soul in love with variety and flexibility. That "escape from ideas" which T. S. Eliot has noted in James is, seen from this point of view, anything but "baffling": it is so deeply rooted in James's vision of life that not a single one of the great mythologies of the age—capitalism, socialism, conservatism, liberalism, Catholicism, Protestantism, feminism, male authoritarianism, Puritanism, hedonism, aestheticism—could hold him.

But it is when we turn to James's fiction that we see most strikingly the incorporation of the passivity-aggression equations of *A Small Boy and Others*. Merely to line up these equations is to see how directly and unvaryingly they are made to inform the fiction. The untyped and unformed observer versus his alter ego, the typed and formed man, the doer, the aggressor; the inconsistent, free, and rootless versus the consistent, fixed, established, or "placed"; the detached versus the attached; the impractical versus the practical; ineffectuality versus shrewdness, know-how, worldly acumen; stillness and passivity versus power, action, energy; tameness versus wildness and passion; the spiritual and inward versus the worldly and external or the hard and functional view of life; the tendency to give up or relinquish versus the tendency to take, seize, get: these are the very terms of conflict in James's fiction. And James's handling of these polarities is marked by a constant ambivalence—as we might well expect, based on the hypothesis that his fiction is the expression of his self-knowledge. For if he accepts that he is what he is and can be nothing else, and if, as artist, he feels proudly that he does "live" in his own way—and live intensely—that acceptance does not preclude his yearning to overcome his temperamental limitations and to give over the reins to his alter ego. More exactly, if he is inclined to side with the ego because of its superior breadth, detachment, openness, and freedom, he is also acutely aware that its passivity and tameness, its inclination to shrink from direct contact, constitute a terrible and dangerous limitation and that (as he remarks in his Preface to the New York edition of *The Spoils of Poynton*) the free spirit is all too often " 'successful' only through having remained free." In a world in which the fittest survive, the alter ego obviously has awesome advantages.

What is most pertinent to our understanding of James's fiction is that the relationship between the two selves is almost invariably seen as that of the hunter and his prey, the trapper and the trapped; and what is equally important is that James presses, whenever the normal probabilities of the situation permit—and increasingly in his later fiction—to effect a reversal of positions, so that the hunter becomes the hunted and vice versa. Much of his later fiction may in fact be viewed as an elaborate paradigm of the situation in "The Jolly Corner," that remarkable story which has inevitably engaged the attention of biographers and critics. The hero in that tale, Spencer Brydon, returns to America to put his property in order and discovers, to his surprise, that he has a "real gift" for practical affairs (17:440)—a mastery so great, in fact, that he falls to wondering what might have been had he remained in America and chosen business as a career. Had he stayed, he feels sure, he would have become "one of those types who have been hammered so hard and made so keen by their conditions"; he would "have had power" (17:449, 450). And, seized by his fascination with his alter ego, he begins to revisit the old house in which he had lived in order to track down his fiercer self. But is he the hunter or the hunted? James plays with the question, and if Brydon at first feels himself to be "some monstrous stealthy cat" prowling after "the poor hard-pressed *alter ego*" (17:458), the tables are presently turned; and it is he who becomes the prey stalked by his alter ego. When at last he confronts the apparition, when he sees "his grizzled bent head and white masking hands, his queer actuality of evening-dress, of dangling double eye-glass, of gleaming silk lappet and white linen, of pearl button and gold watch-guard and polished shoe"—when he sees himself "standing there for the achieved, the enjoyed, the triumphant life," he finds that he cannot face "his triumph"; and as the alter ego advances "as for aggression," the ego gives ground and falls back "as under the hot breath and the roused passion of a life larger than his own, a rage of personality before which his own collapsed. . . ." (17:475, 476, 477). The alter ego, the man of power and aggressiveness, whose life is "larger than his own," triumphs. But the triumph is momentary. In the last scene Brydon awakes and receives, almost as compensation, Alice Staverton's love. The alter ego "has a million a year," says Brydon to Alice, "but he hasn't you" (17:485). Thus, as is usual in James's later fiction, the tables are turned. The reader of *A Small Boy and Others* can scarcely fail to see the connection between these victories of the ego and that early nightmare recounted in Chapter 25—"the most appalling yet most admirable nightmare of my life," as James describes it, and one whose remembrance, upon his awakening, he terms "fortunate" because the memory constitutes one of the "sources at which an intense young fancy . . . capriciously, absurdly drinks" (p. 347):

The climax of this extraordinary experience—which stands alone for me as a dream-adventure founded in the deepest, quickest, clearest act of cogitation and comparison, act indeed of life-saving energy, as well as in unutterable fear—was the sudden pursuit, through an open door, along a huge high saloon, of a just dimly-descried figure that retreated in terror before my rush and dash (a glare of inspired reaction from irresistible but shameful dread) out of the room I had a moment before been desperately, and all the more abjectly, defending by the push of my shoulder against hard pressure on lock and bar from the other side. The lucidity, not to say the sublimity, of the crisis had consisted of the great thought that I, in my appalled state, was probably still more appalling than the awful agent, creature or presence, whatever he was, whom I had guessed, in the suddenest wild start from sleep, the sleep within my sleep, to be making for my place of rest. The triumph of my impulse, perceived in a flash as I acted on it by myself at a bound, forcing the door outward, was the grand thing, but the great point of the whole was the wonder of my final recognition. Routed, dismayed, the tables turned upon him by my so surpassing him for straight aggression and dire intention, my visitant was already but a diminished spot in the long perspective, the tremendous, glorious hall, as I say, over the far-gleaming floor of which . . . he sped for *his* life, while a great storm of thunder and lightning played through the deep embrasures of high windows at the right. [*Small Boy*, pp. 347–49]

For all its helplessness and passivity, the ego can act, can be aggressive; it is not necessarily at the mercy of "the other." Hence the sense of "sublimity," of grandeur. He who had been the prey of the aggressor suddenly shows that he has power of his own and that, far from being the unresisting victim, he is in his own right the hunter. Small wonder that James's imagination drank deep at this brimming well!

In discussing this dream and the problem of the confrontation with the alter ego, most critics have so far focused on a few of James's stories, those in which the alter ego is unmistakably identified by James as alter ego. Yet it requires very little extrapolating, I think, to see that virtually all of his fiction is concerned with just that confrontation. The conflict is developed, in the main, between those worldly people who "know how"—the manipulators, the arrangers, the enslavers, who seek to seize and appropriate everything for themselves—and those innocent and unhardened souls who, unable to operate effectively in the world, can counter the assault of their enemies, their enslavers, only by learning a strange method of resistance: the renunciation and sacrifice of their material interests. James's typical hero is, as we might expect, almost invariably the victim: he is acted upon, he does not himself act until he is driven to the wall by an evil, predacious worldliness. He gives, they take; he renounces, they make the most of their opportunities. Yet again and again the mild, "feminine," helpless victim displays an unexpected strength, and the aggressors, far from looking formidable, are exposed in the end as "small," "sterile," "dead," "old," or cowardly. The victim, neither weak nor enslaved, is revealed as large, virile, youthful, and free.[6] And if, at the end, the hero comes away empty-handed, it is clear that he might have triumphed on his own terms. What prevents him from doing so is both his refusal or inability to accept the world's premises and a moral strength so abundant that generosity is its spontaneous issue.

The permutations of the conflict are, of course, often very subtle, and as I have indicated, the ego is by no means regarded with total sympathy, nor the alter ego with a total lack of sympathy. (There is a sense in which the ego and alter ego are indistinguishable and equally praiseworthy or blameworthy, as I shall show later.) But the essential pattern perdures in tale after tale, from the beginning to the end of James's career. There are, however, some interesting developments in the way James handles the hero's response to aggression. In the early tales the characteristic response tends to be the renunciation of the hero and his removal from the world of action: a sort of symbolic recognition that functioning in such a world, on the terms established by the grasping, active people of the earth, is simply impossible. After 1890, however, the hero's response increasingly exhibits a determination to fight for whatever is at stake in the action—to employ, indeed, all the tactics of the aggressors and to turn the tables whenever the normal probabilities of the story permit. And this shift from renunciation and retirement from life to active fighting testifies eloquently to the change in James's state of mind during these years.

To trace these transformations of plot-structure and symbolism in his fiction is to trace, at one remove, the darkening of

James's vision of life, the progressive deepening of his "imagination of disaster." One witnesses his growing conviction that all of life is a fight and that evil arises even in conduct apparently innocent or noble. Behind apparently benign and unselfish conduct James discerns the shadow of a rapacious egotism, a will to power, an instinct of territoriality. But as he penetrates into this heart of darkness, he continues to work with the passivity-aggression equations of his earliest work; his evaluation of passivity, however, is subtly altered.

In the first place, an apparently innocent and passive victim may be seen to be, in his own way, quite as capable of exemplifying "ferocious and sinister" qualities as are aggressive and active people. Indeed, James discovers that the victim's passivity in the face of aggression, his renunciation or retirement from the battle of life, is also a great evil—a monstrous beast in the jungle. To shrink from the battle, to retreat into some sanctuary of peace and safety, even as the artist retreats into his world of fictions—is this not in truth a desire to regress to Nirvana, to the paradisaical state of the infant, to seek omnipotence in a self-created world, free from all the "responsibility of freedom"? Passivity, then, so far from eliciting sympathy, becomes the strategy of egotists, queer monsters who wish to live effortlessly in the perfect safety of their self-created world, imposing their wills on a static world that offers no threat whatsoever.

In the second place, James develops his imagery and symbolism in such a way as to reveal that the active, aggressive people are really even more "passive" than the inactive. Despite all the ferocity and bullying of the "great active ones of earth—active for evil," their very acceptance of the ways of the world, their surrender to the world, "ferocious and sinister" as it is, is a form of passivity and marks them as stamped-out products of the time-machine of the world or as caged beasts in the great trap of life—the great round material earth, the circus, the show, the *bousculade*. Thus the villains are exposed as helpless in their passivity. And passivity, whether in the victimized ego or in the aggressive alter ego, becomes, I believe, the greatest of evils in James's work, especially in his last novels. Thus, in a surprising way, the counterattack of the childhood dream is repeated in the fiction; and James's work, taken as a whole, becomes a series of paradigms of that dream. But we shall have to look closely at the structure of the novels from start to finish before we can discern the depth and pervasiveness of the pattern.

We begin with the hero or heroine—that divided self whose soul is a mixture both old and new, hedonistic and ascetic, idealistic and worldly, artificial and natural, "European" and "American." To explore the oscillating behavior of such a self and to discern his position in relation to the fixed aggressors who seek to use him and (as L. C. Knights observed)[7] "to thwart the free development" of his life is to follow the adventures of an imagination that circles again and again over the same ground, surveying a landscape that is "endlessly the same and endlessly different." Yet there are significant developments in James's handling of this divided "free spirit." These developments are clearly related to James's own anxieties and to his experiences after 1886, when, as he said to William Dean Howells, he had fallen on evil days. The divided self of the fiction is, at one remove, the divided self of Henry James; and while our concern is always James's imagination, his sense of life, we shall find that a glance at his personal problems immensely enhances our understanding of his art.

2
The Divided Self

> The development of the great writer is the development of his theme—the theme is part of him and has become the cast of his mind and character.
> —Joyce Cary

Critics have often called attention to a significant passage in the Preface to *The Spoils of Poynton* in which James refers explicitly to his creation of "the free spirit" and to the relationship of that spirit to those who surround him:

> . . . Fleda almost demonically both sees and feels, while the others but feel without seeing. Thus we get perhaps a vivid enough little example, in the concrete, of the general truth, for the spectator of life, that the fixed constituents of almost any reproducible action are the fools who minister, at a particular crisis, to the intensity of the free spirit engaged with them. The fools are interesting by contrast, by the salience they acquire, and by a hundred other of their advantages; and the free spirit, always much tormented, and by no means always triumphant, is heroic, ironic, pathetic or whatever, and, as exemplified in the record of Fleda Vetch, for instance, "successful," only through having remained free. [10:xv]

The importance of the passage can hardly be overemphasized.[1] The creation and handling of the "free spirit"—the spirit condemned to "variety of imagination," the "consciousness that was to be nothing if not mixed"—must indeed be regarded by formalist criticism as a necessity of James's art—an inevitable structural implication of James's desire to dramatize the theme of freedom and encagement. For if the artist would reveal sharply the threat to the free spirit, what better strategy than to place this figure between two camps of hostile aggressors, such as "Europe" and

38

"America," to present both aggressors as seeking to "get hold of" the free spirit, and to dramatize the struggle of that spirit to preserve its freedom? Clearly some such structural principle underlies James's art; and his typical plot, character alignments, and imagery may readily be explained in terms of it. But since that struggle of the free spirit and his jailers is always a conflict between "passive" and "active" agents, and since a deep anxiety underlies the characteristic structure of the fiction, one can hardly avoid the conclusion that the creation of the free spirit was not merely an aesthetic necessity; as we noted earlier it was also the expression of anxieties that beset James during his childhood and throughout his life. So we shall be led in the following chapters to refer, from time to time, to the divided self known to psychology—that schizoid personality who feels himself caught in a world that presents, in R. D. Laing's words, a "persistent threat and danger" and who fears that "any impingement" of "the other" will be "total, will be implosive, penetrative, fragmenting, and engulfing."[2] In making use of psychological insights into the divided self, I am of course very far from concluding that James himself was "schizoid" or even "neurotic." There is ample evidence that he had a robust sense of his own identity and worth. But the anxieties described by R. D. Laing and others are not, after all, peculiar only to schizoid personalities. They are felt to a degree by many imaginative people: for example by unquestionably sane people who cannot "throw off the burden of the consciousness of evil."[3] And it seems fair to say that James, in developing his art, made extensive use of his intuition about the anxieties of the divided self. Indeed, James's entire vision of "the great trap of life"—his "imagination of disaster," his sense of life as "ferocious and sinister"—is such a vision as could have been developed only by an imagination saturated with an appreciation of the dilemma of the divided self. Thus the psychological perspective can enlarge immensely our understanding of James's art.

James's concern with the plight of the free spirit is found in a well-developed form as early as 1875, when in *Roderick Hudson* he created Rowland Mallet, a protagonist who is preeminently the unattached man. In his youth, we learn, Mallet has been "passive, pliable, frank, extremely slow at his books and inordinately fond of trout-fishing" (1:13). "He had frequent fits of extreme melancholy in which he declared that he was neither fish nor flesh nor good red herring," James writes, and: "He was an awkward mixture of moral and aesthetic curiosity, and yet he would have made an ineffective reformer and an indifferent artist" (1:16). The mixture of moral and aesthetic curiosity suggests that Mallet is both "American" and "European," that he transcends the limitations of each world. And that suggestion is reinforced by an interesting complication of the plot through which he becomes, quite unknowingly, the third man to whom Christina Light is attracted—neither American artist nor European prince but a man more complex than either of his rivals.

Both Roderick Hudson and Prince Casamassima deprive Mallet of a woman he might have loved. They stand at opposite poles—the poles of nature and artifice—and both are limited. Hudson, unlike Mallet, shows no signs of Bostonian earnestness; he is a product of untamed America. As nature's child—impulsive, wild, amoral, like "some beautiful, supple, restless, bright-eyed animal, whose motions should have no deeper warrant than the tremulous delicacy of its structure" (1:31)—he is incapable of making decisions and sticking to them. He cannot choose; he can only drift "from accident to accident," from experiment to experiment (he believes in "unlimited experimentation"), from impulse to impulse, and from woman to woman (1:262). In the end, he simply dries up. He cannot work, and in the place of his will is "a perfect vacuum" (1:432).

As for Prince Casamassima, the other rival for Christina Light's hand, he is so unmanly that he must be "carried up the Faulhorn in a palanquin," "like a woman" (1:489–90). He sits "upright in an attitude, apparently habitual, of ceremonious rigidity" (1:241). His eye is "dull" and "heavy." If Hudson is all restless experimentation and "undiluted naturalness," the Prince is the stamped-out product of the past, "of pride, of temper, of bigotry, of an immense heritage of more or less aggressive traditions" (1:493). He is at home, not in nature, but only in Rome, "the natural home of . . . the spirits with a deep relish for the element of accumulation in the human picture and for the infinite superpositions of history. . . . the immemorial city of convention" (1:92). If Hudson is enslaved by his impulses, the Prince is enslaved by convention, and the used-up artist is the counterpart of what Mr. Leavenworth calls "one of these used-up foreigners."

So the aggressive rivals for Christina Light are, in truth, impotent. It is Mallet alone who fits Christina Light's definition of "a great character": "the man who's strong with what I call strength . . . would neither rise nor fall by anything I could say!" He is the sort of man for whose sake she "would send Prince Casamassima and his millions to perdition" (*Roderick Hudson*, 1:261). And the crowning evidence of Mallet's strength is demonstrated in the scene in which, fed up with Roderick Hudson's unscrupulous egotism, he turns on the artist in rage and disgust, accusing him of ungratefulness and of unmitigated selfishness. Hudson, astonished by the charges, asks why Mallet has never told him all this before. Mallet replies, "Nothing short of your unwarrantable aggression just now could have made me . . . break my silence" (1:509). And when he adds that he is in love with Mary Garland, Hudson is so overwhelmed by the sense of his own "hideous" conduct that he departs for a walk into the Alps; next day, after a violent storm, he is found dead.

Rowland Mallet does not win Mary Garland; but he does outlast his opponent. Hudson, the man of flashing sensual power, breaks down and dies spiritually before his impulsiveness drives him to physical death. It is the passive Mallet who wins the love of the woman Hudson most desires—Christina Light—and who continues, even to the end, to woo Mary Garland.

Whether he will ever succeed in winning her love is not clear; but we can discern the formula implicit in his characterization, a formula to be repeated over and over in James's fiction. The hero or heroine—at bottom an unattached soul who straddles the two worlds of Europe and America, the old and the new, the artificial and the natural, "aesthetic curiosity" and "moral impulse," whose excellence consists in the largeness and detachment of his view of things, in his freedom and his "acute perception of alternatives"—is set upon by the single-minded, clutching agents of two tyrannical systems that would deny his possibilities and narrow his scope. Driven to the wall by these competing aggressors, the hero may suffer "frustration, pain, loss." But while Sally Sears is certainly right in arguing that the basic pattern of James's work is "the creation and collapse of the fiction [of a world which is the objectification of the hero's desires], its failure," it does not seem to me true that James lacks a "positive vision" or "dialectic of salvation."[4] On the contrary, by making his hero's characteristic response to aggression a refusal to cooperate with the world and to do the world's work, James does affirm. To a degree the hero prevents the world from manipulating him (and his friends) as mere pawns in the great "game of grab" (*Ivory Tower,* 25:35); and he does succeed—increasingly, as we shall see, in the later fiction—in turning the tables on the world's aggressors and in striking a blow for freedom and nonattachment.

This basic structural principle that we have identified in James's novels can be seen by glancing at a paradigm of character construction in the tales from 1877 to the novels of his major phase (see accompanying chart). There are, of course, many complexities in structure and characterization which the paradigm cannot begin to suggest (and the list might be much extended, as well). Clearly, the nature of the "aggression" exhibited by Mr. Longdon or Milly Theale or Prince Amerigo or Adam Verver must be examined carefully and understood in all its uniqueness. (Adam Verver, for example, obviously doesn't threaten Maggie. Yet Maggie is torn between her attachment to Adam and her attachment to Prince Amerigo. Maggie does all she can to preserve her close relationship with her father, but eventually she must cut herself off from him; and she resists his example by substituting compassion for his indifferent use of other human beings. Adam's will, throughout the novel, is virtually absolute; and like Milly Theale, he is always "provoking" because his wealth constitutes an acceptance of the dependence of others on him. We shall look into the nature of Adam's aggression in Chapter 3.) For the present, however, it is sufficient to indicate the persistence of the pattern and to suggest that in laying bare these basic oppositions, we are indeed touching the very passion of James's passion.

In the creation of Claire de Cintré in *The American,* James sharpens his portrait of the divided self, and the competition of the rivals ("Europe" and "America") for the soul of Claire is rendered with the sureness one expects in an artist who perfectly understands the premises and structure of his work. Like her brother, Claire de Cintré is neither "American" (as Professor

Character Construction in James's Work

Title	The Unattached Soul	The Aggressor Attached to the New and Modern	The Aggressor Attached to the Old
Watch and Ward	Nora Lambert	George Fenton, Hubert Lawrence	Mrs. Keith
The American	Claire de Cintré	Christopher Newman	the Bellegardes
"Madame de Mauves"	Madame de Mauves	Longmore	M. de Mauves
The Portrait of a Lady	Isabel Archer	Caspar Goodwood	Warburton, Mme. Merle, Osmond
The Europeans	Gertrude Wentworth, Felix Young	the Wentworths	the Baroness
The Reverberator	Francine Dosson, Gaston Probert	the Dosson family, George Flack	the Probert family
The Bostonians	Verena Tarrant	Olive Chancellor	Basil Ransom
The Princess Casamassima	Hyacinth Robinson	the socialists: Hoffendahl, Muniment, etc.	the aristocrats: Prince Casamassima, et al.
The Aspern Papers	Tina Bordereau	the "publishing scoundrel"	Juliana Bordereau
The Spoils of Poynton	Fleda Vetch	Owen Gereth	Mrs. Gereth
The Awkward Age	Nanda Brookenham	Mrs. Brook	Mr. Longdon
The Ambassadors	Lambert Strether	Mrs. Newsome	Madame de Vionnet
The Wings of the Dove	Merton Densher	Milly Theale	Kate Croy
The Golden Bowl	Maggie Verver	Adam Verver	Prince Amerigo, Charlotte Stant

Poirier has argued) nor "European," but is drawn to both worlds —in fact, is torn between them—so that the imagery used to represent her is inevitably mixed. At the beginning of the action she has surrendered to the Old World, to her mother and Urbain. She has allowed herself to be "sold once." But she has also fought against her jailers over the disposal of her husband's property, and when Newman appears she is again tempted to strike out for independence and "expansion." Her youthful desire for independence wars with her inclination to submit passively to a life-denying tradition:

> She was tall and moulded in long lines; she had thick fair hair and features uneven and harmonious. . . . Madame de Cintré was of attenuated substance and might pass for younger than she probably was. In her whole person was something still young and still passive, still uncertain and that seemed still to expect to depend, and which yet made, in its dignity, a presence withal, and almost represented, in its serenity, an assurance. [*The American*, 2:121–22]

In her "stillness, in her "moulded" passivity, standing serene as "a kind of historical formation," she is the portrait of a lady, the Old World's victim; but her height (the other Europeans in this novel are uniformly short), her slenderness, her uncertainty, and her youth suggest a capacity for independence and expansion. The oppositions implicit in this passage—tall/short, youth/age, the spontaneous/the "moulded," action/passivity, motion/immobility—have already become a habit of James's imagination. The seminal opposition, that of art and nature, is stressed in the 1877 edition. Claire, like Isabel Archer, combines these opposites:

> [Her face] was illuminated with something which, this time at least, Newman need not have been perplexed whether to attribute to habit or to intention, to art or to nature. She had the air of a woman who has stepped across the frontier of friendship and, looking around her, finds the region vast. A certain checked and controlled exaltation seemed mingled with the usual level radiance of her glance.[5]

Even the "exaltation" she feels as she responds to Newman's proposal to make her "perfectly free" is "checked and controlled." And it is a question whether nature and spontaneity or art and control will win out. In the end Claire enters the convent, refusing to accede either to her family or to the aggressive Newman. She cannot bear to side with one party against the other, and she has come to abhor "the hateful miserable world" in which "we *must* give pain (*The American,* 2:417). So she decides to sacrifice herself, leaving the world of the aggressors and giving up "everything."

The "tendency toward renunciation, evasion, indirection, or passive capitulation" that Sally Sears has emphasized in James's work[6] is nowhere more evident than in *The American.* Yet the divided self, as developed in James's fiction, is never completely passive nor does he ever quite capitulate. Part of him is passive and seeks to escape the world of aggressors; another part of him, however, resists the bullying and fights stubbornly for independence. Thus Isabel Archer, in *The Portrait of a Lady,* is tempted again and again to flee from the aggressors, then for a time she passively capitulates to Osmond; yet in the end when she returns to the Palazzo Roccanera her decision exhibits not mere submission but a determination to "live" and fight for Pansy's freedom. So the conclusion reflects the division in her soul that is present from the very beginning, when we see her sitting at Gardencourt with "white hands . . . folded upon her black dress" and note that while her "flexible figure [turns] itself easily this way and that," her smile is "a clear, *still* smile" (3:21; emphasis mine).

Readers who do not understand Isabel's final choice in this novel are misled because they fail to see the division in Isabel's nature. She is "very fond of [her] liberty," and we learn that as a small girl she protested against the "laws" of the primary school (*Portrait,* 3:24, 29). Yet the "elation of liberty" has been coupled with the "pain of exclusion" from the school in which "childish voices" are heard "repeating the multiplication-table," and for all her adventurousness, she has "never opened the bolted door" of the "office" in which, as a child, she secludes herself— that "chamber of disgrace for old pieces of furniture" (3:29–30). What is it then that she wants—liberty or laws, originality or repetitions and copying, motion and quickness or a bolted prison full of mouldering furniture? Is she, as Ralph Touchett affirms, "very natural," or (as he also observes) is she a "Titian" (3:58, 86)? She herself hopes to bridge the gulf between appearance and reality, artifice and nature: "her life should always be in harmony with the most pleasing impression she should produce; she would be what she appeared, and she would appear what she was." Yet in James's most deliberate summation of Isabel's character, it is the "mixture" and the "combination" in her that is stressed:

> Altogether, with her meagre knowledge, her inflated ideals, her confidence at once innocent and dogmatic, her temper at once exacting and indulgent, her mixture of curiosity and fastidiousness, of vivacity and indifference, her desire to look very well and to be if possible even better, her determination to see, to try, to know, her combination of the delicate, desultory, flame-like spirit and the eager and personal creature of conditions: she would be an easy victim of scientific criticism if she were not intended to awaken on the reader's part an impulse more tender and more purely expectant. [*Portrait*, 3:69]

The spirit is "desultory" as well as "flame-like"; and her "infinite hope that she should never do anything wrong" may be a noble desire for perfection, but it may also be the social animal's fear of the *faux pas*, the trepidation of a timorous "creature of conditions" who is determined to "look very well." Isabel, like all of James's free spirits, is divided; a part of her is indisputably "American," yet to Americans she appears "foreign."

The division in Isabel, manifested scores of times in her desire to surrender to the security of the world and in her opposite desire to soar above the earth in a beautiful freedom, reappears in the portraits of Verena Tarrant and Hyacinth Robinson in the two novels James published in 1886. Verena, in *The Bostonians*, is indeed a rather mechancially conceived and rendered version of the divided self; and the plot of the novel, executed according to the blueprint James had prepared a decade earlier, is a mechanically worked-out version of her struggle between two aggressors. She is drawn both to Olive Chancellor, a suffragette and a proponent of modern liberalism and cold renunciation, and to Basil Ransom, a Southerner and a reactionary, devoted to "his pedigree" and to "Bohemianism." Verena is both "like Esmeralda" and "like an Oriental."[7] She likes both the "earnestness" of Boston and the "epicureanism" of New York. And so she oscillates between the two aggressors until she is eventually caught and caged.

Yet Verena is hardly more than a repetition of the heroines

James had been creating for a decade. In creating Hyacinth Robinson in *The Princess Casamassima*, however, James was able to introduce a fresh complication into his portrait of the divided self. As many critics have observed, the division in Hyacinth Robinson's nature is explicitly traced, in the manner of Zola, to heredity: "There was no peace for him between the two currents that flowed in his nature, the blood of his passionate plebeian mother and that of his long-descended, supercivilised sire. They continued to toss him from one side to the other; they arrayed him in intolerable defiances and revenges against himself. . . . " (6:264). Hyacinth—like the other characters in this novel—is all contradictions. His name itself is a contradiction, both exotic and plain. Even more ironic, the exotic name, "Hyacinth," turns out to be that of his plebeian mother's father (who was, we learn, a "republican clockmaker"), while the plain name, "Robinson," is the pseudonym of his aristocratic father, Lord Frederick. From the plebeian he gets the aristocratic name; from the aristocrat, the plebeian.

Equally contradictory are his physical characteristics, symbolic of the division of society into two camps, the high and the low. His mother having been "at the very bottom" of the heap, Hyacinth is inevitably stunted—"no bigger than a flea," says Pinnie (*Casamassima*, 5:10, 18). Yet his curly hair clusters "round a forehead which was high enough to suggest remarkable things" (5:79). His profession also points to the central contradiction. Art and drudgery, the exotic and the mean, the refined and the coarse, are fused in the bookbinder's craft: ". . . the uncovered flame of the gas . . . lighted up the ugliness in which the hand of practice endeavoured to disengage a little beauty—the ugliness of a dingy belittered interior, of battered dispapered walls, of work-tables stained and hacked. . . ." (5:325). Indeed, Hyacinth finds so many contradictions both in himself and in the world, that he cannot determine whether he is "plunging or soaring" (5:297). He is "*ab ovo* a revolutionist," but he is "not a bit democratic" (5:342; 6:38). And if he sometimes thinks of himself as a "barbarian" or a "codino" (as Mme. Grandoni calls him), he remains incorrigibly a gentleman; "You haven't a vulgar intonation," the Princess tells him, "you haven't a common gesture, you never make a mistake. . . ." (6:131, 60).

So he is drawn to opposites: to Millicent Henning, the plebeian who suggests "majesty," and to the Princess Casamassima,
the princess born a commoner—a "radiant angel" who is like "a
loose Bohemian, a shabby adventuress" (6:160, 329). And if he
serves the revolution (a movement composed of plebeians who
wish to rise), he is also drawn to the world "even as it is." But
whether it is the high or the low that attracts him, Hyacinth
Robinson realizes at last that he is in a world in which people
only seek to "get hold of" him and use him for personal gain.
And, buffeted by a score of disillusionments and betrayals, he
commits suicide.

Thus, up to 1886, the hero in James's fiction is incapable of
launching any sustained counterattack against the aggressors of
the world. James's heroes, to this point, are indeed so young and
plastic that they cannot deal with experienced, determined aggressors: James cannot invent plausible means by which "helpless
plasticity" would defend itself and fight back; the canon of verisimilitude requires that the hero fail in his struggles to resist.
And James was not quite ready—he was still too genial—to forfeit
some of the reader's sympathy by exhibiting the hero's use of
coercive tactics.

Between 1886 and 1900, however, James was to find means of
representing aggressiveness in his heroes and heroines. In this
period James's vision darkens: he is no longer willing to attempt,
as in *Portrait,* to awaken a "more tender" impulse in the reader.
He is determined to make his fiction tougher, more "naturalistic."
In 1884 he writes to William Dean Howells affirming that the
French naturalists "do the only kind of work, to-day, that I
respect," and James goes on to say:

> . . . I regard you as the great American naturalist. I don't think
> you go far enough, and you are haunted with romantic phantoms
> and a tendency to factitious glosses. . . . the said gloss being a
> constant defect of *my* characters; they have too much of it—too
> damnably much. But I am a failure!—comparatively. Read Zola's
> last thing: *La Joie de Vivre.* This title of course has a desperate
> irony: but the work is admirably solid and serious. [*Letters,* 1:105]

James was a failure—comparatively—because he had blunted the
edge of his analysis, his "scientific criticism." Thus he came to
see Isabel Archer as "ghostly," and in 1898 he declared that he

had "bloodier things *en tête*" than *The Portrait of a Lady* (*Letters*, 1:279). He was also coming to see, as he says in letters to A. C. Benson and H. G. Wells, that "it is *all* a fight," that life is "all a grind and a bloody battle" (*Letters*, 1:253, 298). And as he launched his campaign to win success in the theater (the success that would give him perfect liberty), he wrote to William in 1893: "But à la guerre comme à la guerre. I mean to wage this war ferociously for one year more...." (*Letters*, 1:211). In a world of warriors, he sees himself as fighting like the others to annex his "little province"—even if it is as small as "the grand Duchy of Pumpernickel" (*Letters*, 1:253).

In *The Princess Casamassima* and *The Bostonians*, James's vision of predation and enslavement had been extended to everyone *except* the hero.[8] But in *The Tragic Muse* James takes a great step. Even his unattached hero is seen as working to coerce others into his own little system. Indeed, James is so determined to view all of his characters without "factitious glosses" that he is willing, apparently, to forfeit sympathy even for the "free spirit." In this icily conceived and icily executed novel, which James described as his most "carefully written" to that date, Nick Dormer is analyzed with perfect detachment; James's "scientific criticism" is remorseless. Indeed, therein lies the great fault of the novel: Nick's emotional involvement in the conflict—the upheavals and turmoils of his soul as he tries to break away from Julia Dallow and the political life—are never adequately dramatized. The novel is worked out cerebrally, and one never feels that Nick is ever more than a tepid or (as James feared) a "purely whimsical personage."

But the forfeiting of sympathy for Nick was, to a degree, made inevitable by James's desire to tell the "full ironic truth" even about his hero. A number of critics have misunderstood Nick's nature and his role in the novel; he has repeatedly been classified as an artist who, like Miriam Rooth, is opposed to the "life political, the world of public affairs."[9] But the truth is that like all of James's heroes and heroines, Nick is hopelessly split between two alternatives. By his own admission, Nick is "two quite distinct human beings, who have scarcely a point in common" (*Tragic Muse*, 7:244), a man "conscious of a double nature." There are "two men in him, quite separate, whose leading features had little in common and each of whom insisted on having an independent turn at life" (7:260). Peter Sherringham observes that Nick is "neither fish nor flesh" (8:106); Miriam Rooth says that he isn't "anything." He desires power and position—and he desires to paint. He does not want to appear a fool in the world, yet he is strange. So his fate is precisely what Gabriel Nash predicts: "You'll eat your cake and have it, and every one, beginning with your wife, will forget there's anything queer about you, and everything will be for the best in the best of worlds. . . ." (8:406). At the end of the novel Nick is painting, to be sure, but he is painting Julia Dallow, the political woman, and all indications are that he will marry her. Thus Nick's division of soul, his inability to choose between art and politics, is contrasted with the unswerving dedication of Peter Sherringham and of Miriam Rooth to their vocations. Peter and Miriam may be attracted each to an opposite way of life; but when the chips are down, there is no question of what each of them will do: Peter, unalterably the diplomat, will not sacrifice his career even for Miriam Rooth; Miriam, unalterably the artist, would not dream of giving up her career in order to become the wife of a great political or diplomatic leader. Peter follows his special line and as a reward for his constancy gets "a superior appointment" (8:440). Miriam plays her "individual pipe" and is rewarded, at the end, by becoming a great artistic success. But Nick Dormer compromises, and whatever "success" he may have at the end is unquestionably tainted by that compromise. Nick, it is apparent, has been "recaptured" by Julia Dallow; his future is predicted in Gabriel Nash's speech:

> She'll get you down to one of the country-houses, and it will all go off as charmingly—with sketching in the morning, on days you can't hunt, and anything you like in the afternoon, and fifteen courses in the evening; there'll be bishops and ambassadors staying—as if you were a "well-known" awfully clever amateur. Take care, take care, for, fickle as you may think me, I can read the future. . . . [*Tragic Muse*, 8:406]

Nick, it seems likely, will become an "awfully clever amateur"—not precisely an unpleasant life, but then scarcely a noble one either; and we may doubt that it will be a particularly happy one. Thus James's divided hero is once again condemned to frustration in a world inhabited chiefly (as Gabriel Nash points out) by the "unregenerate"—those who want others to "join [their] little camp or religion, get into [their] little boat," those who "hate you" if you refuse to become a convert to their religion or a citizen of their empires. The way of the world is the impressment of others into these little boats.

And if in politics there is always this insistence on joining the party, on the absolute power and sovereignty of the "camp," the world of art is no different: the theater, too, constitutes a religion and an empire, an old and established cult, and its votaries must surrender themselves utterly to the authority of the "little temple of art." Not only do Julia Dallow and Mr. Carteret seek converts; Madame Carré and Mlle. Voisin of the Théatre Français are equally single-minded in their dedication to their "church" and "temple" (7:354). And, as in *Casamassima,* we find ourselves in a world in which enslavement is the law of life, and freedom—resistance to all the traps laid by the aggressors—is known only to the man who refuses to participate in the battle, a Gabriel Nash.

The significant development of *The Tragic Muse,* however, as I have indicated, is that the divided Nick Dormer is not a purely passive victim of this world. He is hardly as far removed from the world as Gabriel Nash, and so he plays, from time to time, much the same game as the single-minded aggressors who strive always to get others into their boat. Early in the novel we see him saying to Gabriel Nash, "I should like to get hold of you" (7:27), and again, "I'll go anywhere with you so that, as I've told you, I mayn't lose sight of you—may keep hold of you" (7:59). In order to keep hold of Nash, Nick promises to do anything his friend tells him to (7:54), but he makes exactly the same promise to Julia Dallow (7:109), and it is a mark of his divided nature that he does not really know whom he wants to obey—or whom, should we say, he wants to get hold of. In the love scene that takes place in the temple of Vesta, we see him trying to take "possession" of Julia Dallow; as Biddy says, "Nick has tried to hold her, but she has wrested herself away" (8:107). In his studio, at the end of the novel, we see him still "clinging" to Gabriel Nash and trying to "catch" him in a sketch (8:408–9). Nick has no trouble whatever capturing the image of Miriam Rooth or that of Julia Dallow. To these models he can always say, "Don't move—don't move!" and they will obey. But Nash proves uncapturable. The image that Nick draws has "an odd tendency to fade gradually from the canvas" (8:412). And Nash is a most uncooperative model: he dislikes "the homage of a directer attention than he had ever had" (8:410); he resents being "interpreted. . . . From being outside of the universe he was suddenly brought into it, and from the position of a free commentator and critic, an easy amateurish editor of the whole affair, reduced to that of humble ingredient and contributor" (8:410). So after the first few sittings, Nash simply disappears. He remains, to the end, a "merman," "wandering free" or "floating" (7:169, 27); he refuses to become one of the "doers," competing with others for the rewards of the material earth.

Is Nash, then, as Leon Edel claims, the voice of wisdom, the perfect exponent of James's views?[10] In a sense he is: his resistance to the imprisonment of the world stands as a noble affirmation of moral independence. But to stand outside the universe is to be as queer as that "queer monster, the artist." Nash may be, as he says, "eternal"; he is certainly not part of the temporal world of clocks and mechanisms; but when he melts into the elements at the end of the book, it is hard to believe that he represents the "ideal." Those who play the world's game and do the world's work may not be admirable; but to be a totally "free spirit" is to remove oneself from the universe altogether. That removal may also constitute a trap. In any event, Nash's membership in the "Club Anonymous" is not presented as an ideal, only as a vivid contrast with the way of the world. At this point in his career James was moving toward a very skeptical view of a free spirit who declines to enter the area of action. Here we touch on a major shift in James's attitude toward his most sympathetic characters.

After 1890 James would never again gloss over the element of the "ferocious and sinister" in his "free spirit." And indeed he questions whether such a spirit is, or can be, "free." He is increasingly aware of the "darker and unapparent [life], in which things *really* happen" (*Letters,* 2:105), aware (as Dorothea Krook has observed) that "the selfless motive is inseparable in experience from the selfish, the beneficent action from the acquisitive. . . ."[11] During the nineties James develops an irony as devastating as it is subtle: the behavior of the hero or heroine, however sympathetic that figure may be, is seen as essentially no different from that of the unsympathetic characters. Aggression, duplicity, and the manipulation of others are discovered in almost all of James's characters. James does not abolish the distinction between sympathetic and unsympathetic characters, nor does he ever lapse into moral relativism. Yet he moves steadily toward the sort of psychological perspective, spawned by French naturalism, that regards the psyche as the product of "necessity," condemned to work out the "terrible algebra" of its fears and desires.

It will be sufficient for our purpose here to glance at two works of the nineties before we proceed to examine the handling of the divided self in James's last novels.

Critics have disagreed sharply in their interpretations of the heroines of *The Spoils of Poynton* and *The Awkward Age.* Perhaps nineteenth-century conceptions of the heroine continue to distract us from evidence that points to an unsympathetic view of their characters, and it has not been recognized that in creating Fleda Vetch and Nanda Brookenham James was continuing to explore the predicament of the divided self. Yet once we recognize that predicament as central in these novels, most of the difficulties of interpretation are, I think, easily removed.

Fleda Vetch is indeed complex—if she is not distressingly simple! Seen sympathetically, she is (as F. W. Dupee, Pelham Edgar, and half a dozen other critics have argued) a noble young woman who brings her "crusading spirit" into the lives of Mrs. Gereth and of Mrs. Gereth's son, Owen; Fleda risks her "natural happiness" in order to "exercise the moral sense," checking her desire with a hundred delicate scruples. Seen unsympathetically, she is no more than what James refers to, a bit contemptuously, in his Preface as his "moved manikin" and a "mere little flurried bundle of petticoats": she is a self-deluded egotist consumed by vanity and desire, a "hungry girl" who is perhaps a bit of a "leech" and a "parasite," a "stiff little beggar" who can view herself in her presumption as a princess or queen, a priestess at the high altar of the exquisite, the tasteful, the delicate. But to get a balanced view of her we must see both of these sides simultaneously and recognize that like Emma Bovary, Sister Carrie, Mme. Loisel, or like James's telegrapher in "In the Cage," Fleda is a creature trapped by circumstances, condemned to a mean or drab existence and driven compulsively to seek a compensation, an escape, in her idealizations, in her dime-novel romancing, her sentimentalism, her irrepressible daydreams of the perfect man and the high-toned life. That is why she is called "Fleda": she flees from reality.[12] Yet at every turn her idealized or romanticized view of things is undercut, contradicted by stubborn facts: by instincts and motives which are anything but noble, by her desire for the spoils, a desire to rise and gain preeminence, by a response to "the things" so intense that it amounts virtually to worship and brings to mind (as James remarks in the Preface) "brazen idols and precious metals and inserted gems in the tempered light of some arching place of worship" (10:xii).

The strange logic of Fleda's life dictates incessant oscillations between idealism and acquisitiveness, between a romantic and a practical view of things. Thus she is, in a sense, Nick Dormer all over again: she would have her cake and eat it too; she would live in the world and yet live above the world, unsullied by its sordid compromises. She would maintain a high view of herself as sublime, but she would also get hold of the spoils of Poynton and rise, regal and splendid, like her mentor, Mrs. Gereth.

It is precisely this inability to follow a consistent line of action that James apparently had in mind when he described Fleda as "the free spirit" of the novel—that spirit which is "always much tormented, and by no means triumphant," a spirit "heroic, pathetic, or whatever, and 'successful' only through having remained free." A number of critics, puzzling over this passage and over the fact that Fleda does not seem so much free as self-deluded, have concluded that James either departed from his announced intention[13] or, in his preoccupation in the Preface with technical concerns, forgot the "realities of the book" he had written.[14] Yet it seems unlikely that any writer whose grasp of his art is as complete as James's would forget what he made or that viewing his novel in retrospect, he would formulate an intention essentially different from the one he had held in the act of composition. The remark about the free spirit must be accepted, therefore, as a formulation of what James refers to in the Preface as a "general truth" about fiction—a principle describing the structure not only of *Spoils* but also of all of James's major fiction. Take a free, an unattached, a divided person, James says in effect, and subject him to the pressure of the enslaved, the attached, the single-minded people of this world. The free person won't be successful in worldly terms: free people never are. The spoils go to the hard, functional people, the efficient ones, the Mona Brigstocks or the Mrs. Gereths. But, James concludes, there is the interest—in the conflict between the uncommitted spirit and the enslaving world.

If this is a fair indication of what James meant in the Preface, then we might expect to see in *Spoils* an exhibition of the same sort of structure we have glanced at in the earlier novels: that is, the placing of the unattached, unconsolidated spirit between two opposites, a representative of the Old World and a representative of the New, and the dramatizing of their struggle for possession of the free spirit. And, in fact, close attention to the motif of seizure and possession, as it is developed in *Spoils,* discloses that Fleda is, as she sees herself, in danger of being possessed by two people: the domineering mother, Mrs. Gereth, whose passion for collecting and whose perfect attachment to objects old and exquisite stamp her as the representative par excellence of the Old World; and the son, Owen, who hasn't an aesthetic nerve in his body, is happy in the vulgar modern world, and whom Fleda associates with "the earth and the weather"—as if he were "all potent nature in one pair of boots" (10:150). To say that Fleda is torn between art and nature, or the Old World and the New, is to oversimplify, yet the polarities are present as the germ of James's character-construction and plotting; and there is no doubt that Fleda's incessant reversals and oscillations in the novel are due, above all, to her fear of being possessed, encaged, by either the mother or the son. We shall look more closely at this fear later.

Fleda's efforts to have her cake and eat it too end in a pathetic defeat. She loses the spoils of Poynton (and Owen), but she clings, in her penury, to Mrs. Gereth. Losing the cake, she accepts Mrs. Gereth's dole of crumbs; and to the end Fleda tries to idealize her dependent condition, maintaining the fiction of a lofty independence and an exquisite superiority.

The nature of Nanda Brookenham, in *The Awkward Age,* has also provoked critical debate. Nanda may appear to be "in moral ascendancy" at the end of the novel, and it is possible to view all of her relationships with others as animated by her moral sense, which, presumably, has been quickened by contact with Mr. Longdon.[15] Yet F. W. Dupee has argued that Nanda's moral sense is "bleak by contrast with the world's radiance" and that "the daughter invites final judgment as little as does the mother."[16] And the claim for Nanda's "moral sense" is unquestionably challenged by a number of incidents pointing to her duplicity and self-seeking. For example, there is Vanderbank's condemnation of her conduct in Book Tenth, and there is Nanda's admission to Longdon: "I *am* like that"—"like what he [Vanderbank] thinks" (9:543). In effect she acknowledges that she has an ineradicable taint of modernity and a bad conscience. Thus while she says she has married Mitchy to Little Aggie in order to "save" them both, we can scarcely fail to observe, as Mitchy explains to Vanderbank, that his marriage to Aggie "gets me . . . out of the way" (9:372)—"it just disposes of me, doesn't it?" (9:312). With Mitchy "out of the way," Vanderbank is unable to offer, as a reason for not marrying Nanda, the pretext that he cannot deprive her of Mitchy's fortune. And with Aggie, the girl Vanderbank loves, out of the way, Nanda would seem to have Vanderbank "squared" for herself. Moreover, Nanda's acceptance of Mr. Longdon can be interpreted, from Vanderbank's point of view, only as her acceptance of a crushing bribe. Once Mitchy has married Aggie and once Vanderbank has shown himself unable to take Longdon's bribe to marry Nanda, Longdon is all that Nanda has left.

The fact that she has all along been playing a careful game for high stakes is suggested in half a dozen passages. There are, for example, the recurrent references to her extraordinary omniscience, to her tact and discretion (9:376, 410), to the fact that she does not "show" what she wants (9:396). Above all, as proof of Nanda's desire for gain and power, there are the references to her accumulation of possessions as she comes gradually into Longdon's favor. At Longdon's house, in Book Fifth, we see her standing "with an air of happy possession" as she surveys "the high walls that were so like 'collections' " (9:203, 204). When she sees Vanderbank, she handles his cigarette case and after rubbing her cheek "with the polished silver," tells him, "This is the kind of one I should like" (9:208). Later, we see her handling an "old snuff-box" and gazing at the "curious handle" of Mitchy's umbrella (9:359, 528). And we learn that she dresses so well that she arouses her mother's envy: she is "feathered and ribboned, dressed in thin fresh fabrics and faint colours" (9:315); she has "long soft gloves, which one of her hands again and again drew caressingly through the other"; and her parasol is "a more delicate thing much than any one of [her mother's]" (9:318, 320). Finally, there is the representation of her room in Book Tenth, the room to which she has given so much "study of effect"—the room which prompts Vanderbank to exclaim, "You *have* got a lot to show!" and Mitchy to chorus, "How charming you've made your room and what a lot of nice things you've got!" (9:494, 514). Has Nanda, then, like the idealizing Fleda Vetch, a concealed desire to "gather in the spoils"? The implication seems inescapable. When Harold declares that Nanda is "working Mr. Longdon, like a good true girl" (9:391) and observes cynically that it certainly is not Longdon's company that is wanted but the best possible price he can give, Nanda accepts the idea of gain even as she repudiates the cynicism: " 'If he hears us talking in this way, which strikes me as very horrible,' Nanda interposed very simply and gravely, 'I don't think we're likely to get anything' " (9:394).

There is much additional evidence to suggest that Nanda is not what she seems; but we have seen enough, I think, to warrant our concluding that Nanda is precisely what James took her to be—the fruit of "compromise." If she is surprisingly an example of "the moral sense," she also remains what she has been made: a creature who, like her mother, can plot and scheme with furious industry to achieve her ends. Like Mrs. Brook, she accepts that she is part of "the circus—it's the way we earn our living" (9:189). But as F. W. Dupee has pointed out, she lacks the openness, the spontaneity, the animal warmth, and the vitality of youth that distinguish her mother. If Mrs. Brook is youth itself, investing even the "hardest teachings of life" with "childlike innocence," Nanda is "old Nan," and at the end of the novel we learn that she might have been . . . a very much older person than her friend [Mr. Longdon]" (9:289, 544). Thus the modern daughter turns out to be the oldest person in the book, not only because she is attracted to the "beautiful" past but also because she invariably shows all the tact and prudence of experience. Indeed the central paradox of this hourglass novel is that Nanda, the modern daughter, becomes old and learns the ways of the Old World—the world of the Duchess, who makes no concessions to freedom but follows unquestioningly the Continental arrangements for the disposition of her young Aggie—while Mrs. Brook, who is "youth" itself, who is indeed no more than a "baby," finds her place taken by her daughter. At the end of the novel it is Nanda who has gathered about her, for consultations, many of the members of her mother's circle; it is Nanda who is worrying about her mother, while Mrs. Brook is youthfully beginning all over again.

The division in Nanda's soul, then, is a division between the Old World and the New—between Longdon and Mrs. Brook. Neither the Old World (as represented either by Longdon or by the Duchess) nor the modern world (as represented by the horde of carnivorous people romping in the ring of the London circus) is "free"; both worlds seek to take hold of "helpless plasticity" and to mold it for their own ends.[17] Pride, rapacity, and self-seeking are everywhere in this wasteland—as in the wasteland of *What Maisie Knew*, where Maisie Farange, like Nanda, is seen both as a product of the world and as an opponent of it. The divided self, caught in such a world, makes such adjustments as it can; and in its division it is both "heroic" and "pathetic."

As he turned to the writing of his last novels, James's consciousness of the "awful mixture in things" (*Golden Bowl*, 24:292) —and the awful mixture in his heroes and heroines—was obsessive. In Nick Dormer, in Nanda Brookenham, in Maisie Farange, in Fleda Vetch, he had uncovered unsuspected duplicity and aggressiveness. He was aware too—as Dorothea Krook and others have observed—that the highest virtue and the noblest development of human capacities are linked to "corresponding" weaknesses and derelictions. As he said in a letter to R. W. Chapman in 1912:

> What one has done has been conditioned and related and involved —so to say, fatalised—every element and effort jammed up against some other necessity or yawning over some consequent void—and with anything good in one's achievement or fine in one's faculty

conscious all the while of having to *pay* by this and that and the other corresponding dereliction or weakness. [*Letters*, 2:242–43]

James's consciousness of how he himself had "paid" was acute. "Alack, alack," he writes to Gaillard T. Lapsley in 1908, "how we do have to pay for things—and for our virtues and grandeurs and beauties . . . as well as for our follies and mistakes" (*Letters*, 2:92). And to Edith Wharton in the same year, James wrote: "Life is terrible, tragic, perverse, and abysmal. . . . Ah, I'm conscious enough, I assure you, of going without, and of all the rich arrears that will never—for me—be made up—!" (*Letters*, 2:91–92). The list of his deprivations must have lengthened as he grew older: his loneliness; his ignorance of business and finance; his flight from sexuality; his fear and timidity; his basic unworldliness. "It takes one whole life," he writes to Charles Eliot Norton, "—for some persons, at least, *dont je suis*—to learn how to live at all. . . . " (*Letters*, 1:337). And he was even conscious of his inability to do many of the things as an artist he would have liked to do. Thus to H. G. Wells he writes, apropos of the latter's criticism of "The Turn of the Screw": "Bless your heart, I think I could easily say worse of the T. of the S., the young woman, the spooks, the style, the everything, than the worst any one else could manage. One knows the most damning things about one's self" (*Letters*, 1:298–99). And to Howard Sturgis's observation that no one would understand *The Awkward Age*, James replied: "I tell *myself*—and the 'reviews' tell me—such truths in much cruder fashion. But it's an old, old story—and if I 'minded' now as much as I once did, I should be well beneath the sod" (*Letters*, 1:318). He confesses, in effect, that he cannot help himself—that he is the victim of his temperamental limitations, his fastidiousness, his taste for "ambiguities," his detestation of "great glares" (*Notes . . . Brother*, p. 106).

In his creation of the heroes and heroines of his last novels, it is, then, the "fatalised" condition of these divided spirits that he stresses. Their freedom is their "necessity"; they are "condemned" to freedom. But freedom to "live" in a world of aggressors now implies not passive capitulation but active fighting and counteraggression. As in the early fiction, all of the protagonists in the novels of James's major phase are initially passive victims practiced upon by active aggressors; but all launch concerted counterattacks against these worldly bullies, and all turn the tables. Becoming even more aggressive than the cruel gladiators of the social arena, they enslave the enslavers and force the active ones into a condition of helplessness and "surrender"—a state of total passivity. Thus Milly Theale and Maggie Verver supersede the women who have tried to use them and win the love of the men attached to those women. Lambert Strether refuses to knuckle under to Mrs. Newsome, asserts his independence, and by the end is not ambassador but a sovereign in his own right, one to whom Maria Gostrey and, to a degree, even Chad and Madame de Vionnet "surrender."

In each of the novels of this period (as in the earlier fiction), a protagonist is placed squarely between the "old" and the "new." Strether in *The Ambassadors* stands between Mrs. Newsome and Madame de Vionnet—between the rival empires of Woollett and Paris. Maggie Verver in *The Golden Bowl* is bound both to her father, Adam, and to Prince Amerigo—to the immensely wealthy and powerful American collector and to the scion of the Old World. The situation in *The Wings of the Dove,* however, is more complicated. Milly Theale is divided in the sense that she stands between the "Alps" and the "labyrinth"—between her desire to perch above the world and her desire to participate actively in society—but that is not a division between the old and the new. It is Merton Densher (whose fate becomes as important as Milly's after Book Fifth) who is here divided between "America" and "Europe"—between the American heroine, Milly, and the European antagonist, Kate Croy. Thus James introduces, as an additional complication of the figure in the carpet, a divided self who is unsympathetic and who stands between two women, the immemorial fair and dark heroines. And the same pattern is found in *The Golden Bowl,* where Prince Amerigo stands between Maggie Verver and Charlotte Stant. We shall see presently that the histories of Densher's and Amerigo's vacillations and their oscillations between the radiant American and the *femme du monde* constitute a rich completion of James's vision of the plight of the divided self.

The Wings of the Dove illustrates strikingly James's recasting of the elements of his fiction in all of his later novels. The heroine, Milly Theale, is, like Isabel Archer, the uncommitted creature of possibilities—"the potential heiress of all the ages," as James calls her (19:109), a young woman capable potentially of enjoying either "boundless freedom" or of submitting passively to her inheritance and allowing herself to be chained in the labyrinth of the world. Milly's "freedom" is always, to a degree, illusory: she is swept along by the current of the past, by her position and her wealth. She "cannot get away from" her money, and, as James points out in the Preface, her hands are "imbrued too, after all, in the measure of their never not being, in some direction, generous and extravagant, and thereby provoking" (*Wings,* 19:x). So she is inevitably a prisoner of the invidious material world; and from the beginning, when she stands in the Alps "looking down on the kingdoms of the earth" and "in a state of uplifted and unlimited possession" (19:124), her situation is ambiguous. She may indeed be the dove, in her "uplifted" state, but she is also the empress of the material earth. She is the "provoking" heiress whose wealth is in effect an acceptance of the dependence of others upon her: precisely the condition James's father condemned in the letter James quotes in *Notes of a Son and Brother.*

Milly eventually throws off her passivity, descends from the Alps, and enters the world. The "idea of a great adventure" seizes her, and in London, on a walk through the slums, she sees herself as shouldering "some queer defensive weapon, a musket, a spear, a battle-axe . . . demanding all the effort of the military posture" (19:248). Reacting against the vision of herself as the portrait of a lady—"dead, dead, dead"—she begins to "live" (19:221). So the mild dove becomes a warrior and commences her counter-attack on the world that has sought to force her into "a current determined," so that "'not she but the current acted" (19:274). She supersedes Kate Croy and wins Densher's love. She spreads her wings and, paradoxically, the invidious world is found "nestling under them."

Divided in the sense that her temporal power and her spiritual aspirations are contradictory, Milly would be one of James's most interesting heroines if her inner conflict were dramatized more effectively. After Book Fifth, however, James's interest in the divided self focuses not on Milly but on Merton Densher, whose divided condition *is* dramatized. And it is Densher, finally, whose fate provides the real center of the action.

He too is the passive, unconsolidated hero whom others have "got hold of" and who, by the end of the action, is, like Isabel Archer, both free and chained. Again, he is rather like Rowland Mallet: "detached" and "awfully at sea" (19:52). He looks "vague without looking weak—idle without looking empty."

> He suggested above all, however, that wondrous state of youth in which the elements, the metals more or less precious, are so in fusion and fermentation that the question of the final stamp, the pressure that fixed the value, must wait for comparative coolness. And it was a mark of his interesting mixture that if he was irritable it was by a law of considerable subtlety. . . . One of the effects of it was that he had for you surprises of tolerance as well as of temper. [*Wings*, 19:48–49]

Densher is the son of a "British chaplain" and a woman who "copies . . . famous pictures in great museums" (19:92, 93). So the possibility of his turning in either of two directions is suggested: he may seek spiritual elevation—the heights of the dove —or he may become one of those who, like Gilbert Osmond, are mere copies and copiers—stamped out by the world's, by convention's, crushing dies. The division is strongly suggested in the observation that "through his descent to English earth, he had passed, by the way, through zones of air that had left their ruffle on his wings—he had been exposed to initiations indelible" (19:93). He reminds one of Conrad's Lord Jim after the jump from *The Patna*.

Unlike Jim, however, Densher makes no effort to keep himself afloat in "the destructive element." He is totally passive, he lets Kate Croy do everything. Or if he shows any signs of action, they are but tokens of his sexual "necessity"—his desire to possess Kate and to "play on" her (20:8). But submission to such necessity is also, of course, a form of passivity, and even his sexual aggression is passive: Kate must come to him.

Yet Densher is a reluctant participant in the plot to "work" Milly. Indeed he is so disgusted by the world of grab—the so-called civilization, the "social boom" of the London "arena"—

that he takes up "again his sense of independence," thinking: "He had supposed himself civilised; but if this was civilisation—!" (20:43, 44). So he oscillates between Kate and Milly; always "doing nothing," he is swept along in the current (20:77, 80). When Kate tells him that he is "free" to do what he wants, he cannot act (20:93) but he resents her manipulation of him, his being placed "where he was" and taken as "a thing accepted in mere helplessness." He asks himself whether he has "no will left" (20:177). And so he begins to walk "round and round" in his apartment, turning like the turning world.

Eventually, ashamed and sickened by his role in the plot to get Milly's money, he admits, "I *am* dead" (20:272). And like Maisie Farange he concludes that "it was of himself he was afraid" (20:282). Then Milly, seeing his plight and doing everything to purge him of his shame, advises him to leave Venice. And eventually he is "forgiven, dedicated, blessed" by her.

In love with the memory of Milly and in an altered state of mind as Christmas dawns, Densher feels "somehow determined." His "determined" condition here suggests choice, *self*-determination: "He acted . . . in the sense of that marked element of the rare which he felt to be the sign of his crisis. And that is why, dressed with more state than usual, and quite as if for church, he went out into the soft Christmas day" (20:352). Yet his action, his decision, is inseparable from "his necessary course," which remains "to follow Kate" (20:361). Turning his moral dilemma over to her, he asks her to consent to the surrender of Milly's fortune. She is the one to make the final decision. "I do nothing," he says; he desires only to "escape everything" (20:400, 402). And Kate, forced to choose between Densher and the money, states her condition: she will marry him if he will swear that he is not in love with the memory of Milly. But Densher, divided to the end, cannot swear.

Thus the divided self, viewed unsympathetically, remains passive. The divided self, sympathetically conceived, throws off passivity and turns the tables on the active ones. Only in the world of action—within the limits of "necessity"—is "freedom" possible. It is precisely on these premises that James was to construct the characters and the action of *The Golden Bowl*.

I indicated, at the beginning of this chapter, that the fiction, viewed from a psychologist's perspective, reflects many of the anxieties of the schizoid personality. In the first chapter of this study we have seen that James saw himself as condemned to the taking of life "indirectly" and to a "restlessness of envy" toward the active people who go in for life "directly" and energetically. But we are in a position to look further. What we witness in the fiction is the slow shift in James's attitude toward his passivity— a shift expressing a desire to overcome the ego's normal inhibitions and thus to release the latent aggressiveness of the alter ego. And we see in James's own life a growing revulsion, a growing contempt, for the passive condition of the mere observer and recorder of experience. In the early fiction the passive hero is treated with deep sympathy, and James desires to elicit a "tender" feeling for him rather than to subject him to "scientific criticism." But as his career unfolded, James seems to have recognized not only that such passivity is contemptible but also that it is a mere mask and that, in the depths of the soul—that darkness where things really happen—his own aggressiveness was ferocious. Thus in contemplating his critical avidity, he employs the same vocabulary he was to assign to the aggressive and predatory narrators of *The Aspern Papers* and *The Sacred Fount:*

> To criticise is to appreciate, to appropriate, to take intellectual possession, to establish in fine a relation with the criticised thing and make it one's own. The large intellectual appetite projects itself thus on many things, while the small . . . projects itself on few.
>   Admirable thus its economic instinct; it is curious of nothing that it hasn't vital use for. [11:xix]

And if the critic, ostensibly the free spirit, is driven by an obsessive acquisitive instinct, what of the artist? Percy Lubbock observed of James: "He was insatiable for anything that others could give him from their personal lives. . . . it was as though he feared to leave them to inexpert hands and felt that other people could hardly be trusted with their own experience" (*Letters*, 1:xvii). The intensity of his "clutching instinct" could scarcely have gone unexamined by James. Had he not written in 1871 that England would "yield its secrets only to a really *grasping* imagination" (*Letters*, 1:30); and had he not seen clearly his own aggressive tendencies during the playwrighting period, when he wrote to William that he meant to "wage this war ferociously" (*Letters*, 1:211)? Like the narrator of *The Sacred Fount*, James was a man driven by "the habit of observation" and possessed by an idea: a man avidly grabbing, and fitting whatever he could grab into his system. The artist may write about the glories of freedom and spontaneity, but is he ever himself, in his most passionate celebrations of his idea, anything more than the slave of his obsession, his compulsion to create and become God of an ordered universe?

In the later fiction we see James turning, then, against himself—subjecting his ego to the sort of scientific criticism and withering irony that he had spared Isabel Archer. He turns, especially, on his ineradicable passivity. He had begun, as I have pointed out, by presenting his hero-victim with deep sympathy: it was the aggressive takers and manipulators, those who "knew how," who were evil. And yet the victims, the passive ones, were they not, viewed critically, mere cowards who fled—little Fledas—whenever aggression loomed before them?

Here it is illuminating to consider the change in James's handling of the escapist tendencies of his protagonists. In the novels before 1890 James evokes pity for the protagonist who escapes from the clutches of the "flagrant worldings": for Claire de Cintré in *The American,* who, threatened by an aggressive suitor and an aggressive family, escapes into the dark convent of the Carmelite nuns in the Rue d'Enfer; for Isabel Archer, who, threatened by an aggressive suitor, wishes to "case" herself in "brown holland," like a piece of unused furniture, who craves "a cool bath in a marble tank, in a darkened chamber, in a hot land" (*Portrait* 3:232, 4:391); for Catherine Sloper, who retreats to the safety of Washington Square; for Hyacinth Robinson, whose suicide carries Isabel Archer's desire for utter peace to its logical conclusion; and for Verena Tarrant, who flees to Cape Cod—"a land of dreams," "the Italy of Massachusetts, . . . the drowsy Cape, the languid Cape, the Cape not of storms but of eternal peace"—before she is seized by the male aggressor Basil Ransom. But in the nineties a sharp irony deeply qualifies the pity we might feel for such a protagonist. Both the caged telegrapher of "In the Cage" and Fleda Vetch of *The Spoils of*

Poynton are presented as sentimentalists and idealists who again and again take flight into a world of dreams:

> She dodged and dreamed and fabled and trifled away the time. Instead of inventing a remedy or a compromise, instead of preparing a plan by which a scandal might be averted, she gave herself, in her sacred solitude, up to a mere fairy-tale, up to the very taste of the beautiful peace she would have scattered on the air if only something might have been that could never have been. [*Spoils,* 10:44–45]

Fleda is not James, neither is Isabel Archer, nor any of the host of characters who manifest similar inclinations in the fiction. But the phrase "in her sacred solitude" (the phrase is "sentient solitude" in the 1896 edition) suggests the connection between the Fleda Vetches of this world and a detached observer who spends a lifetime building his palace of thought. If the soul is threatened by "the other" and unable to compete on practical terms, it can choose to live in a world in which there is no question of competition—a world of fantasy, a house of fiction. We arrive, thus, at the preoccupations that were to produce *The Sacred Fount.* What seizes James's attention in that book is precisely the effort of a passive onlooker to make himself invulnerable by locking up life in his categories, his theories. Encased in his house of fictions, hiding from all real threats, such a person creates a fantasy world in which he has absolute control and forces all the creatures in his universe to do his bidding. He is perfectly safe in this self-created world; nothing will occur in it that he does not wish; and in the imagination, his desire for omnipotence may be gratified at the expense of the aggressors who have driven him into his "sentient solitude."

It seems fair, at any rate, to say that James saw his own inclinations to escape for what they were. After the dreadful repudiation he suffered before the hoots and catcalls of the *Guy Domville* audience, he could say that he preferred to be solitary (*Letters,* 1:248). And he had no illusions about what Lamb House represented in those dark days: it saved him from "the fiery furnace of people" (*Letters,* 1:243). In a sense, then, he had retreated like Isabel Archer to an "office" full of furniture. Or like Adam and Maggie Verver he had retreated to a place like Fawns—a place "out of the world," with a "pleasant hush" and a "serenity."

Or like Marcher in "The Beast in the Jungle" he had curtailed "his liabilities and exposures" and had adopted a strategy of "base safety and shrinkage."[18] But we see James's repudiation of such inclinations most clearly in his letters. He was not one to spare himself; nor, I think, did he like his shrinking ego; and we find him in his correspondence turning on himself again and again with a savage impatience.

In 1911 he writes to Edith Wharton saying that her "beautiful genius" is "so for great globe-adventures and putting girdles round the earth. Mine is, incomparably, for brooding like the Hen, whom I differ from but a syllable in designation. . . . " (*Letters*, 2:198). Again and again the words *craven, pusillanimous, shrink,* and *cower* recur in reference to his attitudes. From the "political bear-garden" he "pusillanimously" shrinks. He finds the circus and the *bousculade* of London "a thing to fly from" (*Letters*, 1:256). The spectacle of "material and political power" is "calculated to make one crouch, ever afterwards, as cravenly as possible, at Lamb House, Rye. . . . " (*Letters*, 2:48). Yet such passivity, such shrinking from the battle of life, he is aware, is fatal. There is no rest, no refuge; and the temptation to fly from the battlefield is not only ignominious, it makes possible the triumph of the Mentmores, the Newmarches, the "bloody billionaires," the "active ones, active for evil." So James turns, in the three novels of his major phase, against his passive hero-victim, subjecting him to incessant irony and compelling him to bestir himself, to fight back, to become even more successful in his aggression than the unregenerate. To carry out their "sacred purpose" in a world which is the devil's, his heroes must act— sometimes even "diabolically"—to control and dominate others. Only through fighting does freedom acquire meaning; it is in the great trap of action that one must seek one's freedom.

In his own life James seems to have tried to heed this lesson. His journey to America in 1904 was at least in part a form of aggression, an effort to bestir himself. He writes to William in 1903:

> Simply and supinely to shrink [from going to America]—on mere grounds of general fear and encouraged shockability—has to me all the air of giving up, chucking away without a struggle, the one chance that remains to me in life of anything that can be called a

movement: my one little ewe-lamb of possible exotic experience, such experience as may convert itself, through the senses, through observation, imagination and reflection now at their maturity, into vivid and solid *material,* into a general renovation of one's too monotonised grab-bag. [*Letters,* 1:417]

In 1904, having taken the great step, he writes to Edmund Gosse:

I have moved from my own fireside for long years so little (have been abroad, till now, but once, for ten years previous) that the mere quantity of movement remains something of a terror and a paralysis to me—though I am getting to brave it, and to like it, as the sense of adventure, of holiday and romance, and above all of the great so visible and observable world that stretches before one more and more, comes through. . . . [*Letters,* 2:20]

And seven years later in a letter to Mrs. Frederic Harrison, it is interesting to observe, he again italicizes the word connected with inaction: "I can no longer stand the solitude and confinement, the *immobilisation,* of that contracted corner [Rye] . . . and I fled to London pavements. . . . " (*Letters,* 2:203). The advent of the world war might compel him to denounce "all the *active* great ones of the earth, active for evil, in our time (to speak only of that,) from the monstrous Bismarck down!" (*Letters,* 2:377). Yet his sense of "the paralysis of my own power to do anything but increasingly and inordinately *feel*" afflicts him (*Letters,* 2:466), and it seems to him that "the happiest, almost the enviable . . . are the younger doers of things and engagers in action" (*Letters,* 2:413). He tries to act, however; and his visits to the wounded in the hospitals, his naturalization as a British subject would seem to be evidence of his fight against passivity.

It seems fair to say that writing fiction helped James to contemplate, and so to work out, the "terrible algebra" of his own life. But like any first-rate artist, he was able to extrapolate from merely personal problems, to generalize his personal predicament. Thus the dilemma of the divided self is the dilemma of all of those who, like Santayana's last Puritan, still cling to what is left of conscience and a sense of sin in a world that has delivered itself up to the experiment of total secularism; it is the dilemma of all who have struggled with the idea of "freedom" in an age in which overwhelming numbers of converging facts suggest a rigid determinism; and it is the dilemma of those like Hamlet who confront a world in which fair appearances seem to mask nothing but "abysses of shadow." All of these great subjects and a hundred more are dissolved into James's fiction, and they are all the inevitable extension of the figure in the carpet. But if we would witness the most remarkable articulations of that figure, we shall have to look even more closely at James's work. Remembering Northrop Frye's remark that our clearest perception of a writer's "meaning" is to be found in the structure of his images,[19] we turn next to the dominant clusters of images and symbols in the novels written between 1875 and 1909. Once again, we discover that James's imagination moved steadily toward the densest expression of the theme of freedom and encagement.

3
Warfare and Aggression

Life *is,* in fact, a battle.   —Henry James, "Ivan Turgenieff"

When Henry James said in 1907 that "the imagination incurably leads a life of its own," we may suppose that he had in his mind's eye a vivid picture not only of the plot structures, the character alignments, and the imagery and symbolism his imagination had already shaped, but also of the life his imagination would lead in his last works. For thirty years he had been developing the vocabulary by which his vision of life might be presented—a vocabulary that would permit him to render in virtually every sentence, and with maximum expresssiveness, the ambiguities of experience in an enslaving world. Every image and epithet would flow from the center, the imaginative source; not a word would arise accidentally. And it was because he now had so complete a grasp of what he could do in his art—of what he wanted every word to do—that he had created virtually a new style. He was determined to make every word vibrate with the energy of the central vision: he would "fish out every little figure and felicity, every little fact and fancy, that can be to my purpose" (*Notebooks,* p. 318).

But how is it possible for the critic to trace the adventures of that unitive imagination? James's imagery and symbolism are so prolific, they flow in so many different directions, that the very abundance would seem to condemn criticism either to an impressionistic superficiality or to the sort of pedantic classification that, instead of bringing us closer to an appreciation of James's art, pulls us further and further away from his central artistic purposes and his central vision. One can only be grateful for the work of Alexander Holder-Barell and Robert L. Gale, who have

70

examined James's imagery with the utmost care and have told us much about the habits of James's imagination.[1] The focus of this study, however, is the unitive nature of James's imagination, and my aim is to determine both how James's images and symbols articulate his central vision of life and how they acquire maximum expressiveness in the concrete wholes in which they appear. In this undertaking, criticism must guard carefully against the creation of a "myth of isolation." Our effort must be to seek out the principles that determine the nature and structure of each work and then to ascertain how the imagery and symbolism flow from the informing principle. The study of structure in James's work, presented in the preceding chapter, is a prerequisite to this examination of his imagery and symbolism.

We are helped immeasurably by the fact that James's imagination is indeed unitive. Thus in the process of dramatizing the threat to the free spirit, James employs again and again the symbol of the cage, together with its symbolic associates—traps, boxes, confining rooms, nets, webs, locks, chains, collars, bridles, girdles, walls. The imagery and symbolism of seizure, of aggression, of war and predation, of touching, handling, pushing, pulling, grasping, clutching, and holding are inevitably evoked by his vision of a threatening world of enslavers. The imagery of immobilization, petrifaction, and quietness is required to define the condition of the enslaved person. Since the enslaving world is one of base, deceiving appearances, James is driven to develop an immense vocabularly relating to acting and "showing" and to all bright surfaces, fronts, and exteriors, as contrasted with the invisible and the inner worlds and with the honesty and spontaneity of "nature." Because the enslaving world is corporeal—a world of mass and extension, one in which only quantities and money and precious objects count (and in which people too count only as "objects" or "values")—he develops an elaborate vocabulary relating to commerce, finance, numerical reckoning, and quantification. Because it is a world imperiously demanding conformity, propriety, endless repetitions of conventions, James develops a vocabulary to designate the mere product or cliché or stereotype, the medal or coin stamped out by a machine. Because the world tries to cramp and confine the soul within narrow boundaries, he develops a vocabulary of shrinkage and smallness to designate its constrictive powers. And so his imagination proceeds, working continually with the central conception of the threat to the free spirit and paying particular attention to the irony that a world apparently civilized, beautiful, radiant, vast, and promising is in truth but a darkness, a jungle, an abyss or a labyrinth, a circus, a machine, or, like Mrs. Lowder's London house in *The Wings of the Dove*, an "office . . . [a] countinghouse . . . [a] battlefield . . . [a] scene . . . of action" (19:30).

To follow James's imagination as it develops these basic motifs is to realize that "the order, the form, the texture" of his novels are, in the words of Vereker, a "complete representation" of his central vision, as well as a triumph of "patience" and "ingenuity." In the end, in novels like *The Ambassadors* and *The Golden Bowl*, James felt that he could write page after page of "rarest perfection"—pages in which every item of experience is saturated with the informing idea. But the density of these novels was made possible only by a lifetime of labor; the creation of a vocabulary adequate to express everything that the vision embraced was gradual. And yet to follow the peregrinations of James's imagination from book to book is to realize, too, how extraordinarily consolidated his vision was from the very beginning. And we shall see as well that all of the richly expressive images and symbols of the late works are clearly anticipated in the early ones.

The appropriate starting point is the imagery and symbolism of warfare and aggression—an inevitable consequence of the pessimism James voiced when he wrote to A. C. Benson that he, James, had "the imagination of disaster" and saw life as "ferocious and sinister." James's pessimism reflects a vision that many of the most influential thinkers of his age—Schopenhauer, Darwin, Spencer, Ricardo, Marx, Loeb, Nietzsche—had made persuasive; but like any man of imagination, James was quick to see beyond the idea of the struggle for survival, scientific mechanism, and the blind will to live. He saw that the struggle could be waged in a hundred ways scarcely dreamt of in the philosophies of Marx or Darwin: indeed, James saw that every item of experience might be taken to illustrate the ferocious fight for survival. He was entirely serious when he wrote to Benson, "It's *all* a fight . . . the only thing that changes is our fighting train" (*Letters*, 1:253). James had recognized that even he, the man condemned by temperament to take life "indirectly," was a fighter, both as artist and as critic, in the great war of life. In a hundred ways he saw—and with a subtlety as acute as that of the French novelist Nathalie Sarraute—that human beings seek safety, invulnerability, and that all of one's faculties are in the service of this overwhelming desire. Thus the prolonged, searching efforts of active and alert intelligences to get at the truth behind the ambiguities of experience and behind the masks that others wear in self-defense are efforts directed toward acquiring the knowledge that will insure safety. And normal experience, in James's work, becomes nothing more than a series of maneuvers by which one person seeks advantage over another, works incessantly to break down the defenses of those who oppose his will, forces others to "surrender," or places them in positions from which any opposition becomes impossible—"squares" them or "fixes" or "holds" them.

It is in examining these strategies of conquest and self-defense that we come closest, I think, to understanding the texture of life in James's fiction—the very process of experience as reflected in James's vocabulary, in the moment-to-moment interplay of his characters, and in his construction of scenes and complications. It is this interplay that I wish to emphasize in this chapter; and I am particularly interested in the kinds of "pressure" that aggressors exert upon the free spirit and in the intimations of the threat of seizure in the language and actions James uses to create the scene. As we proceed, however, it will become obvious that the vocabulary of warfare and aggression blends with, and is finally inseparable from, the symbolic motifs we shall be examining in the next two chapters. Thus the imagery of finance and commerce, which reflects what James calls in *The Ivory Tower* "the awful game of grab" (25:35), obviously extends the idea of seizure and aggression and designates a form of warfare. Similarly, the imagery of appearances and of the eyes focuses on seizure and on fixing and immobilizing a threatening "other." Finally, the imagery of petrifaction, quietness, and the cage is employed to emphasize the condition of victims of the world's aggression. But for the present, let us focus on the imagery of direct aggression and warfare.

The active effort to seize, hold, and direct others is, as we might expect, characteristic of those like Mrs. Lowder and Mrs. Gereth, who act from a position of strength and whose "crude complacency of power" is founded on wealth, success, or social position; but it is also found in the less successful who have will and determination. Both Americans and Europeans fall naturally into this camp, and we have seen that typically both are engaged in a struggle for domination or possession of the free spirit. Robert L. Gale, in his chapter "A Bristling Quiver," has called attention to a number of the war images in James's fiction and has noted that James "viewed human relationships as battles very often indeed."[2] But here we may profitably expand those observations, directing our attention to warfare and aggression in the broadest sense and taking note of many associates of the war images.

The battle of aggressive rivals for dominion is established early in James's fiction. In *The American*, for example, we find Christopher Newman, the "muscular" and "powerful" American, with a "readiness for aggression or for defense" (he has "come out of the war with a brevet of brigadier-general" and looks like "a grenadier on parade"), laying siege to the "stoutly-guarded" Hotel de Bellegarde, in which Claire de Cintré is immured by an unyielding tradition and conservatism (2:25, 3, 59). In *Washington Square* we find both the imperious Doctor Sloper and the imperious aunt, Mrs. Penniman, whose dress, like armor, "always gave forth a sort of metallic ring" and who "marched about" as she seeks to direct Catherine Sloper's life; Gordon Wright of *Confidence* gives "marching orders" and the phrases in his letters "march in stout-soled walking boots."[3] Caspar Goodwood of *Portrait of a Lady* is "plated and steeled, armed essentially for aggression," while Lord Warburton, his English rival, shows an admiration for Isabel that seems to her "an aggression almost to the degree of an affront" and suggests the warlike both in his name and in his boots and hunting crop (3:143). Madame Merle is "armed at all points. . . . her weapons were polished steel, and she used them with a skill which struck Isabel as more and more that of a veteran" (4:154). Then there is Paul Muniment of *The Princess Casamassima,* with his "big strong fists," his face suggesting "a rank of bristling bayonets," and "the glance of a commander-in-chief"—and with a name that denotes a battlement (5:114, 119). Or there is Miriam Rooth of *The Tragic Muse,* whose ambition for success makes her "almost dangerous," like a "tigress about to spring" or a "devouring demon," or like "a young warrior arrested by a glimpse of the battle-field"—a warrior who asserts that hers can only be "a fighting life" and who, we learn, had "a great battle with her fellow-workers and . . . routed them utterly" (7:26; 8:250, 353, 242–43). Or there is Nick Dormer, "perpetually in the field" or contemplating "the battle . . . to be fought" (8:144, 389). There is Nick's mother, Lady Agnes, who "marches" people about; there is Julia Dallow, striding with her "whip" about her "wide kingdom" and imperiously giving orders to others; there is Peter Sherringham, who has a "plan of campaign" and who, as he goes after success in the diplomatic world, "refurbished his arms, rubbed up his strategy, [and] laid out his lines of defense" (7:313). Further illustration is unnecessary: by the time he wrote *The Tragic Muse* James sharply saw all of life as a battle, and the imagery of warfare and aggression is after this date applied to all of his characters, heroines and heroes included. "The roar of the siege and the thick of the fray"—these become the world of society, become life itself—and all of James's characters are potentially what Mrs. Lowder is: "a projectile, of great size, loaded and ready for use" (*Wings,* 19:32, 169). Small wonder that James liked to read biographies of military campaigners!

The vision of life as warfare is developed, as one might expect, in images and symbols designating the application of force in a variety of ways. Very prominent is the great cluster of images having to do with handling, touching, grasping, pushing, pulling, directing, clutching, getting hold of others; or with devouring or swallowing victims; or with tracking, hunting, or pursuing prey. The symbolism is obvious in an early work like *The American,* where Christopher Newman is figured as an eagle that may "pounce down, seize [Claire de Cintré] in his talons, and carry her off" (2:112). It is obvious, too, in a novel like *The Spoils of*

Poynton: Fleda Vetch feels herself "thrust down the fine open mouth" of Mrs. Gereth and feels "buried alive, smothered in the mere expansion of another will" (10:209). But the imagery appears also in subtler passages, as when Mrs. Gereth "applied a friendly touch to [Fleda's] hair and gave a business-like pull to her jacket," or when Mrs. Gereth put her "hands on the girl's shoulders and held them" (10:124, 203). Such passages are worked into the novel not merely because they are realistic but because they amplify symbolically the vision of an unregenerate mankind engaged in the sordid business of using, bullying, and manipulating others. The idea of handling or touching others for unholy purposes is extensively developed in all of James's later novels.

It is prominent, for example, in *The Ambassadors,* not only in the opening scenes (which we shall look at presently) but also in the very plot of the novel. Strether is dispatched to Europe to "get hold of" Chad—to rescue Chad from the "wicked woman" who has "got hold of" him. Yet the mission is, of course, abhorrent to Strether, and we learn early that he feels there is in Europe "the exchange of such values as were not for him to handle" (21:129); reluctant to handle others freely, he at first keeps his hands in his pockets (21:110). But as Strether begins to free himself from Mrs. Newsome's grasp, as he begins to act on his own instead of as Mrs. Newsome's ambassador, he actively takes hold of Chad on his own terms: "[Chad] was amazed to find the hand I had laid on him to pull him over suddenly converted into an engine for keeping him still" (22:41). Moreover, Strether recognizes that both Madame de Vionnet and Mrs. Newsome, the imperious rivals, are such consummate specimens of their types, are so perfectly "finished," that, like portraits of ladies, they resist all alteration, all change: Madame de Vionnet is so perfect that "another touch will spoil her—so she oughtn't to *be* touched"; and Mrs. Newsome "won't be touched. . . . she hangs together with a perfection of her own . . . that does suggest a kind of wrong in *any* change of her composition" (22:153, 239). Yet Jeanne de Vionnet seems to him to have possibilities of developing freely; and, foreseeing a marriage between her and Little Bilham, Strether asks Madame de Vionnet to permit the girl to choose for herself. "She's the most charming girl I've ever seen," he says. "Therefore don't touch her" (21:276). It is not until Madame de Vionnet confesses that she is marrying Jeanne to M. Montbron that Strether begins to sense the perfidy behind appearances; and at length Madame de Vionnet confesses to him that her *hands* are "unholy" (22:286).

Still another extension of the imagery of warfare and aggression can be found in James's examination of the effort to seize reality in a formula or theory, an intellectual system. This is the counterpart of the arms and citadels and battlements that James's warriors employ to make themselves invulnerable. To define and to know is, as D. H. Lawrence so often observed, to bully, to seek to dominate. The knower creates a world in which he has absolute control—a world of his own ideas; he jams or forces the facts into his little system so as to preserve its authority—and his own authority as creator. Thus the narrator of *The Sacred Fount* builds the "great glittering crystal palace" of his theory and fights aggressively to keep it standing against the assaults of skepticism and of opposed systems. Financial imagery mingles with the imagery of predation and warfare in the depiction of this effort. Every addition of information becomes "a grain of gold," a "gain," a "profit," a part of the narrator's precious "collection."[4] He senses that something strange is possessing him; he feels that his idea is an obsession and wishes to get rid of it. But like all the others, he is "pursuing in vain." If at one moment Gilbert Long "had us all in hand" (*The Sacred Fount*, p. 325); if at another the apparently mild May Server, with her "terrible little fixed smile," "collars us" and is "on the pounce" (pp. 351, 358); if Lady John is one of those who give "absolutely nothing whatever, who scrapes and saves and hoards, who keeps every crumb for herself" (p. 336); and if, finally, the "apologue" or "parable" of the sacred fount idea is that "one of the pair . . . has to pay for the other," so that Mrs. Briss gets her "new blood" from her husband, by tapping his sacred fount of life—if there are only these vampires and their victims, the narrator becomes one of the worst of the lot. Like the other predatory hunters of the social jungle, he is seen "on the scent" and "on the track" of his idea (p. 329). Repeatedly he "holds" people, prevents them from "escaping"; May Server becomes his "prey"; Briss is like "plastic wax" in his hands (pp. 368, 386). He imagines himself as a "providence" and an "omniscience," and as his pride balloons, he contrasts his own "magnificent awareness" with the "unconscious-ness" of the others (pp. 414, 480). He even imagines himself as a life-destroyer. But if he has the perspicacity to recognize that his theory-mongering is destructive and sadistic, if he sees that "the sacrifice of feeling" is tied up with "the satisfaction of curios-ity," he remains the victim of his obsession. "My idea was yet what most possessed me," he says (pp. 480, 330); the exhilaration of "intellectual mastery," the joy of "determining, almost of creating results," masters him (p. 435). And he is absolute until, at the end, the "sublime structure" is smashed by Mrs. Briss, who presents "her own now finished system" with "her supreme assur-ance" (pp. 489, 493).

This struggle to dominate or "break down" others by forcing ideas or systems upon them is not, however, confined to *The Sacred Fount.* The competition of rival theories is prominent in several novels in which the ambiguities of experience elicit op-posed interpretations that vie for acceptance: for example, in *The Portrait of a Lady* (the interpretation of Osmond); in *The Ambassadors* (the interpretation of Chad's relationship to Mad-ame de Vionnet); or in *The Wings of the Dove* (the interpreta-tion of Densher's relationship to Kate Croy). What we witness in these and other novels is usually the effort of one character to force his interpretation on others and to prevent a rival inter-pretation from gaining credence.

It is when we examine James's handling of the scene, how-ever—his treatment of the interplay of characters—that we see most sharply how the vocabulary of aggression and defense defines the texture of life and articulates James's vision of life. For a characteristic scenic action in James's novels is the persistent, prolonged assault by an aggressor, an assault before which the defender may or may not hold his ground. The defender is "under pressure" and must use his wits to parry the blows of his opponent. And even in scenes that at first blush seem to have little to do with aggression and defense, the interplay of characters will often be found, on close examination, to be shot through with the vocabulary of these maneuvers.

Consider, for example, the first sixty pages of *The Ambassa-dors,* in which Strether meets and quickly becomes the friend of Maria Gostrey. On the surface all is pleasant, and the exchanges of wit and the recognition of affinities bind the two together in a charming and apparently benign relationship. Yet Maria's aggression is apparent from the very first scene, when we learn that her eyes *"had taken hold of* [Strether] straightway, measuring him up and down as if they knew how; as if he were human *material* they had already in some sort *handled"* (21:10, emphasis mine). Seizure, measurement, and handling all betoken Maria's aggression here, and these symbolic motifs are quickly developed in the scene that follows. Maria, who leaves nothing to chance, has looked up Strether's name in the hotel register. Her first words, when she meets him in the street, have the effect of "checking" him: "It was here she presently checked him with a question. 'Have you looked up my name?' " (21:12). And when Strether confesses he hasn't, and acknowledges his sense of the irregularity of such a procedure before the eyes of the hotel receptionist who has seen them "scrape acquaintance," Maria laughs "at the shade of alarm in his amusement" (21:12).

Presently we learn that Maria "led him forth into the world" —such "leading" being associated with the idea of "directing" others, as when Gilbert Osmond directs Isabel Archer's movements in their first encounter. And in the ensuing scene, Strether is entirely on the defensive. His blurted confession that he comes from Woollett again prompts Maria to laugh; when he tells her that she "won't be able, if anything happens, to say [he's] not been straight with [her]," she asks him, "But what do you think of as happening?" Strether then "gazed about without meeting her eyes; a motion that was frequent with him in talk. . . ." (21:15). Maria's eyes fix Strether freely; he must evade her gaze. She "handles" him; he keeps his hands in his pockets.

Divided within himself, Strether half wishes to escape. He confesses that he is afraid she will find him "too hopeless," and he glances "repeatedly at his watch." But Maria does not allow him to evade her or to conceal his scruples:

> . . . Miss Gostrey took him up.
> "You're doing something that you think not right."
> It so touched the place that he quite changed colour and his laugh grew almost awkward. "Am I enjoying it as much as *that?*"
> [*The Ambassadors*, 21:16; original emphasis. For the remainder of this section, all emphasis is mine unless otherwise indicated.]

A moment later Maria directly proposes an arrangement: "I wish you *would* let me show you how [to enjoy]!" (21:17). Strether, hard pressed by this naked proposal, pleads cheerfully, "Oh I'm afraid of you!" But Maria, we are told, "kept on him a moment, through her glasses and through his own, a certain pleasant pointedness. 'Ah no, you're not!' " (21:17). She continues to hold him with her eyes, and Strether confesses that he has fallen "thus in twenty minutes so utterly *into [her] hands.*"

The nature of the threat presented by Maria is undefined at this point, but there are plenty of clues to arouse apprehension. In the next paragraph, Maria tells Strether, "It's a dreadful thing to have to say, in so wicked a world, but I verily believe that, such as you see me, there's nothing I don't know. I know all the shops and the prices—but I know worse things still" (21:18). When Strether asks, "How do we reward you [for showing us Europe]?" we are told that Maria "had her own hesitation"; and Strether "while still thinking over what she had said," again checks his watch (21:18, 19).

The scene ends with Maria's outright question, her outright demand for surrender: "*Will* you give yourself up? [original emphasis]." At this point "poor Strether [heaves] a sigh" (21:20). But Maria, always pressing him, "[takes] over the job . . . on the spot." The besieged Strether, backed against the rampart of the ancient wall that girdles Chester, has, in effect, "surrendered" to the world into which Maria has led him.

The motifs of seizure, handling, and fixation are continued in Chapter 3, where Strether, Maria, and Waymarsh come together. Breakfast, we learn, has been ordered by Maria—as one of the "responsibilities which Miss Gostrey *took over* with an alertness of action that matched her quick intelligence" (21:35). As Maria and Strether wait in the garden, she explains her system of putting Americans through Europe, and wittily, whimsically, tells Strether that she is "working all the while undergound" and that she sends Americans back home "spent," "*passed through [her] hands—*" (21:37). Strether, amused, tells her that he feels "quite enough . . . [her] abysses. Spent!" and thanks her for "the warning." Once again, he is acutely aware of his "collapses" before her. And it is also clear that the energetic Maria is now directing even Waymarsh: "She *had made him breakfast* like a gentleman, and it was nothing, she *forcibly asserted,* to what she would yet *make him do.* She *made him participate* in the slow reiterated ramble. . . . " (21:38). Small wonder that for Waymarsh, Maria is associated with the threat of seizure by hostile foreign powers or religions! To Waymarsh, Maria seems

> a Jesuit in petticoats, a representative of the recruiting interests of the Catholic Church. The Catholic Church for Waymarsh—that was to say the enemy, *the monster of bulging eyes and far-reaching, quivering groping tentacles*—was exactly society, exactly the multiplication of shibboleths, exactly the discrimination of types and tones, exactly the wicked old Rows of Chester, rank with feudalism; exactly in short Europe. [*The Ambassadors,* 21:41]

Waymarsh's fears may seem absurd, but in Book Second, Chapter 1, the imagery confirms our suspicions. Maria, dressed for the theater, reminds Strether of Mary Stuart, the Catholic queen. Wearing a "cut down" dress and a "broad red velvet band" round her throat, and sitting at a table on which "the lighted candles had rose-coloured shades," Maria is part of the world of vivid appearances that have seized Strether's "long-sealed eyes" (21:50). At the theater, too, there is "the very flash of English life," and Strether sees "types" new to him, people to whom "a series of strong stamps had been applied, as it were, from without; stamps that his observation played with as, before a glass case on a table, it might have passed from medal to medal and from copper to gold" (21:53). In this world of vivid appearances—a world in which people have been "stamped out" by convention and materialism—Strether considers that, if people are in "perpetual evening dress," it may be necessary for him "to fight [Chad] with his own weapons": to wear evening dress himself (21:54). So James introduces the idea he was later to develop so luxuriantly in *The Golden Bowl*: the battle is to be fought exclusively with appearances.

There commences, then, a prolonged conversation in which Maria seeks to learn the circumstances of Strether's trip to Europe. The purpose of the scene, from a formalist point of view, might seem to be purely expository. Yet even here we discover an action involving aggression and defense. And Maria's whole effort, seen in retrospect, is not only to "get everything out" of Strether but also to demolish the woman who has already been figured as her rival—the Protestant queen, Mrs. Newsome.

Maria's examination of Mrs. Newsome is devastating, and poor Strether, always divided within himself, falters repeatedly under the assault:

> "And [Mrs. Newsome] is wonderful," Miss Gostrey asked, "for her age?"
> Strether seemed to feel with a certain disquiet *the pressure of it.* [*The Ambassadors,* 21:56]

> . . . And *she forged ahead.* "Have they money?"
> But it was as if, while *her energetic image still held him,* her enquiry fell short. "Mrs. Newsome," he wished further to explain, "hasn't moreover your courage on the question of contact." [21:58]

> With which *she put again* her question. "Has Mrs. Newsome money?"
> This time he heeded. "Oh plenty." [21:59]

> But she had already *taken him up.* "The way it works—you needn't tell me!—is of course that you efface yourself." [21:65]

> "You don't trust me!" *she once more repeated.*
> "Don't I when I lift the last veil—tell you the very secret of the prison-house?" [21:66]

> He blushed for her realism, but gaped at the truth. "You're the very deuce."
> "What else *should* I be [original emphasis]? It was as the very deuce *I pounced on you.*" [21:67]

> Here Strether's comrade resumed *that free handling* of the subject to which his own imagination of it already owed so much. [21:68]

> She *kept him a moment,* while his hand was on the door, by not answering; after which she answered *by repeating her question.* "What do you stand to lose?" [21:75]

By the end of this scene Maria forces Strether to admit that he stands to lose "everything" if he fails in his mission. She does, indeed, as Strether says, "get everything out." Her appearance, her use of her eyes, her persistence, are all part of the enormous weaponry she can draw upon at any moment. Her repeated questions force Strether to answer, to follow her lead—and to see what she sees. Strether's initiation into Europe is thus, to a degree, his surrender; and the entire pattern of development is essentially that of aggression and "collapses."

I have analyzed these pages of *The Ambassadors* at some length because they are typical of scenic construction in James's novels. The aggressor's attack is transparent in "The Aspern Papers" and *The Sacred Fount*. But veiled attacks appear everywhere in the fiction: in the early encounters of Isabel Archer with Caspar Goodwood or with Madame Merle and Osmond; in Hyacinth Robinson's encounters with Millicent Henning or the Princess Casamassima or Paul Muniment; in Verena Tarrant's encounters with Olive Chancellor and Basil Ransom; in half a dozen encounters in *The Tragic Muse*, where everyone but Gabriel Nash plays the game of coercing and bullying. And even the so-called communion in love between Owen Gereth and Fleda Vetch is informed by the pattern of aggression and defense.

Lawrence Holland has observed that the language and action describing the relationship of Fleda and Owen are "steeped in the gestures of seizure, grasped and clasped hands, possession." One might argue that lovers do, inevitably, seize, grasp, clasp, possess; and Holland, like many other critics, does not doubt that the core of that relationship is love. Yet another interpretation suggests itself as soon as we recognize that what really appeals to Fleda is not Owen but rather the idea of love—the idea of romance and a "secret passion." And the truth is that she partly fears Owen— just as she partly fears Mrs. Gereth—because Fleda, a proud girl, cannot endure being possessed or dominated for very long either by the son or by the mother.[5]

The clues to such an interpretation are everywhere. One of them is found in James's early observation that Fleda

> was prepared, if she should ever marry, to contribute all the cleverness, and she liked to figure it out that her husband would be a force grateful for direction. She was in her small way a spirit of the same family as Mrs. Gereth. [*Spoils*, 10:10–11]

It is because Fleda, like Mrs. Gereth, wishes to dominate, to be superior, that she is disturbed when she hears Owen's voice "sing out like a call to a terrier" and has to recognize that "he was conscious only of her being there as for decent service" (10:39, 40). She is confident, however, that, given the opportunity, she will be able to control him, make him serve her. Thus she reflects that she, unlike Mona, would be able to make him "like anything she would have made him do"; and even when she imagines a violent quarrel between Owen and his mother, she still thinks of him as "unaggressive" (10:56).

Fleda is wrong, to be sure. Owen, whose first name means "the young warrior" and whose last alludes to *guerre*, has in his room "such an array of arms of aggression and castigation that he himself had confessed to eighteen rifles and forty whips" (10:59). And in the scene in which Fleda commits herself to his cause, James everywhere stresses the danger of domination. Owen has come to Fleda to get her help in securing the return of the spoils to Poynton. When Fleda learns that Mona Brigstock is "very angry" about the loss of the spoils, she sees immediately that the marriage of Owen and Mona is in jeopardy. And this prospect kindles all her desire—desire both for romance and for Poynton. Standing before Owen "with the dumb exaltation that she felt rising," Fleda is "wound up to such a height" that she speaks in a manner befitting the heroine of a penny romance (10:99). She tells him that she will work the miracle, will make Mrs. Gereth see the necessity of returning the spoils: " 'I'll make her see it, I'll make her see it!'—she rang out like a silver bell" (10:99). But although this speech has the passion and romantic splendor that Fleda has sought to achieve, it has an unwonted effect upon Owen: he proceeds to make love to her. And at this point Fleda, to protect herself, must reverse her field. Although she has already betrayed Mrs. Gereth, she cannot bear to surrender to Owen, and she senses suddenly that she may be trapped: Owen has shut the door of the drawing room, preventing her flight. So she stiffens herself in a posture of virtue that permits her to keep herself safe from the reality of his passion.

> She saw that Owen had now his sharpest necessity of speech, and so long as he didn't let go her hand she could only submit to him. Her defence would be perhaps to look blank and hard; so she looked as blank and as hard as she could, with the reward of an

immediate sense that this was not a bit what he wanted. [*Spoils,*
10:102]

Within moments she feels "his possession of her hand loosen so
that she [is] free again"—and she has the satisfaction of "closing
the door in his face quite as he had closed that of the drawing-
room in hers" (10:103).

Thus she escapes for the time being, but she is safe only as
long as she can idealize. As long as her fancied passion can be kept
under control, she has an advantage. And that is why James uses
the image of the caged bird to symbolize her so-called love:
"Their protected error (for *she indulged a fancy* that it was hers
too) was like some dangerous lovely thing that she had caught
and could keep—keep vivid and helpless in the cage of her own
passion and look at and talk to all day long" (10:108–9; emphasis
mine). Far better, after all, to indulge a fancy of romantic love—
to have an idealized or imagined passion one can always control
and talk to—than to submit to the reality of Owen's "possession."

But Owen's aggression can scarcely be averted. She tries to
control him: she writes advising him "to keep intensely quiet and
take no other steps"; she flees to West Kensington to avoid being
"made . . . over to [him]"; but in her penury, her powerlessness
("she had neither a home nor an outlook—nothing in all the
wide world but a feeling of suspense"), she is inevitably driven to
risk being controlled either by the mother or by the son (10:134,
141, 145). When she meets Owen in London, then, the battle for
domination and possession resumes. Owen is now "delicately
dressed," and for the poor girl who worships refinements, his
appearance gives him "a tremendous pull" (10:150). Still, she
hesitates. She debates whether admitting him to her home will
give him an "advantage"; then she lets him "direct their course
to the door." Fearing, however, to let the fancied passion out of
the cage, she maintains "her constant idea of keeping cool and
repressing a visible flutter" (10:154). Yet she is, as always, incapable of any single-minded action. She wants Owen, but fears
him; she wants Poynton, but doesn't want to do what she must to
get Poynton. So she plays a veering, dodging game of offering herself and then running away. Concealing from Owen the fact that
she has left Mrs. Gereth because the latter insisted that Fleda

"give herself up" to him, Fleda lets him think that she was impelled to leave by her sense of the injustice done to him—that she has "fallen" because "she had acted for him" (10:157). She also lies when she says she has not repeated to Mrs. Gereth the information that Mona will not marry Owen unless the spoils are returned to Poynton. Thus, for a time Fleda's strategy is to do everything possible to make Owen admire her and surrender to her—everything short of surrendering herself. But when Owen, inevitably kindled by all these apparent evidences of her feeling for him, presses close, she again reverses field and, feeling her "heroism meet its real test," tells him sententiously, "Of course you must keep your word" to Mona (10:159, 160).

The same sort of oscillation in her conduct is apparent when Mrs. Brigstock arrives unexpectedly with the intention of "laying her hand on" Fleda (10:170). Fleda, seeing her chance to make Owen "admire her, adore her"—since, she reasons, he will do this "exactly in proportion as she herself should rise gracefully superior"—at first sets out deliberately to move him "to rapture"; and presently she finds herself speaking as if "she had been [Owen's] wife" (10:174). When Owen defends her, "her joy [is] deep within." But then her sense of her superior grace and tact compels her to dissociate herself from Owen's "tone of familiarity" (10:176). Moments later, again reversing herself, she is excited by her opportunity to play a grand role and cannot resist likening herself to "one of those bad women in a play" (10:177)—a remark which naturally drives Mrs. Brigstock from the house. And before Owen leaves, Fleda gives him such a gaze as will at last accomplish his full surrender.

The next day, however, Fleda is full of plans to renounce Owen. She flees from London, fully intending to abandon him and to give up "the fine office of helping him back to his own" (10:179). She will leave him to fend for himself, both with the pious desire that he "should be superior, be perhaps even sublime" and with the slightly impious sense that such sublimity "mightn't after all be fatal" (10:180). As usual, she keeps the door to Poynton ajar, while enjoying the luxury of being "alone" with the secret of her fancied love. When she receives Owen's letter, however, she again changes her mind, rationalizing that "she owed him something for her obvious failure to help him,

with the utmost care—Maggie feels inclined to bolt for her life.
For a time Maggie is forced to endure Charlotte's "direction":
"Charlotte's hand, promptly passed into her arm, had already,
had very firmly drawn her on" (24:245). But Maggie, at this
point, is quite a match for the militant aggressors; she has learned
to use the weapons of her adversaries, and her transformation
from the prim and proper "nun" to the commander on the field
is, in fact, one of the chief sources of power in this plot.

Thus, after the adultery at Matcham, when Maggie receives
her first intimations of "realities looming through the golden
mist," she plunges into the social whirl, takes over functions
hitherto relinquished to Charlotte, and is "figured . . . as the
relieving sentry" (24:32). Presently, we learn, Maggie has "taken
the field," and Amerigo and Charlotte, returned from their "un-
usually prolonged campaign" at Matcham, discover that "agitated
lambs" may be more dangerous than lions (24:32, 128). Maggie
becomes a "timid tigress," "crouching"; and in her new-found
power she is able to "drive" the others "like a flock of sheep."
She "captures" the attention of Charlotte and Amerigo, who,
confronted by the sudden aggression, are "paralysed"; for Maggie
now has "a grasp of appearances" and can "jam" appearances
"down into their place" so as to compel the adulterers to surrender (24:52).

Maggie sees what she has let herself in for: she knows that
to fight evil she must become "a little beast" (24:209). But it is
precisely her willingness to submit herself to the warlike conditions of the world—instead of escaping to the protective "hush"
of Fawns—that arouses all our sympathy and admiration. Immensely stirring, then, is her challenge to the apparently invulnerable Charlotte and Amerigo as they stand on the "battlements" or on the "rampart," looking down contemptuously at
their challenger (24:99, 143). Maggie must wage a "high fight"
to break down those walls (24:143). She becomes "commander
of a siege" with "prodigious effect . . . at her command"
(24:214, 233). It is she who assumes "control" of the future
(24:236). She can destroy the adulterers easily, and there is
always "that fascination of the monstrous, the temptation of
the horribly possible" (24:233). But she manages to escape the
"beast" of the temptation, and after enduring Charlotte's last,

desperate counterattack, it is Maggie who becomes the "pursuer," who first "guardedly [tracks]" her stepmother in the great house, who then tracks her into "the hard glare of nature" (Charlotte has exchanged "the protection of her room for those exposed and shining spaces"), and who finally seizes Charlotte like "some captured fluttering bird pressed by both hands to her breast" (24:235, 310, 284, 308, 317). Maggie triumphs, then, not by squeezing the bird to death but by letting it go—letting Charlotte think that she has won. So Charlotte returns intact to the world of social animals: she looks splendid and "official"; but she is, resignedly, Adam Verver's domesticated animal, played out on the "long silken halter looped round her beautiful neck"—a superb beast, but a perfectly docile one, being led to her "doom," though she does not, in her bestial ignorance, "so much as know what it is" (24:287).

Charlotte is scarcely the only doomed beast, however, in the jungle of society. Colonel Assingham, whose vocation as soldier is an obvious token of the warlike society, is seen making a "reconnaisance" about the drawing room and, like a "commandant," checking the "fastenings" on the protective windows (23:365). We see him too "during his . . . prowl"—this "Attila" who delights in violent speech because "bad words . . . could represent batallions, squadrons, tremendous cannonades and glorious charges of cavalry" (23:64). As for his wife, the aggressive Fanny, who delights in managing, money, and match-making, her pleasure in nosing out people's secrets is a predator's pleasure in seizing and holding: "I'm getting hold of it," she says with relish, referring to her vision of the effect of the adultery on Maggie. She delights in "mastery" of her subject; she "conquers" an obscurity (23:399). Poor battered campaigner of the social wars, she has not been provided with a "fixed base" for the season, but she is quick to see that at Fawns "the ground she could best occupy" is "her being moved . . . by the admitted grossness of her avidity. . . . " (24:121).

Meanwhile, behind all of these military operations stands Adam Verver, a sort of five-star general whom nothing touches— or a sort of Krupp, who makes the whole show go. When we first meet Adam at Fawns, James sounds the note of acquisitive power and bellicosity in the word *push*. "A spectator in the field" would observe "the push he had applied" to open the door and "the push, equally sharp, that, to shut himself in, he again applied. . . . " (23:125). In his youth, Adam, like "Cortez," has seen "that a world was left him to conquer"; "to rifle the Golden Isles had . . . become the business of his future" (23:141). To accomplish this, he "had to *like* forging and sweating, he had had to like polishing and piling up his arms" (23:144). But having triumphed, he now wishes only to protect himself from the world's aggression, and it disturbs him that he has a "fight" on his hands to protect himself from such warriors as Mrs. Rance and the Lutches, who are bent on his "conquest" (23:209). So he has "need of defenses"; he must wear "shielding glasses" (23:132, 89). Yet in other ways he remains on the offensive. To increase his collection he must go out on his "customary hunt for the possible prize," must risk "life, health, and the very bloom of honour" in his "prowling after precious things" (23:213, 214). It is not enough for him to have "grabbed everything, fixed everything, down to the last lovely object for the last glass case of the last corner"; he must still be "up and doing," and at the end we see him not only continuing to "walk about to review his possessions" but also using Charlotte, whom he has all along treated as a mere object, to attest to his "rare power of purchase" (23:90–91, 360). At Fawns, then, he becomes like the ringmaster of the circus: the "bedizened performers of the circus [are] poured into the ring" and Adam wanders about in the background, always in charge (24:289). In the end he will return to American City to preside over his vast collection—and over the menagerie who come to view it.

In this analysis of the pattern of aggression and defense in *The Golden Bowl* and in the rest of James's work, I have made no mention of the wit, the charm, the comedy, the redeeming human qualities that might compel critics to qualify an interpretation of James's pessimistic vision. What I have stressed is what James called, in the Preface to *What Maisie Knew*, the "*full* ironic truth" of the fiction. If we are to understand James's sense of life —and the texture of his fiction—it is this truth that must be emphasized. Close attention to the pattern of aggression and defense in James's work leads us to some significant revisions of generally accepted views of many of the characters and, in fact, of the "meaning" of the novels. The interpretations developed here of Maria Gostrey, Fleda Vetch, and Adam Verver are in several respects different from those usually propounded by James's critics. And if I have neglected or minimized the more sympathetic elements in the characterization of these people, it is because those aspects have been amply explored, while the aggressive nature of these characters has often been overlooked. In seeking a balanced view of James's fiction, we must always recognize the *"full* ironic truth" about his characters.

What emerges most sharply to me from such a study as this is James's perfect coldness, his perfect detachment, as an artist. For a long time it was virtually taken for granted that James's views of his heroes and heroines were almost unqualifiedly sympathetic and that James's vision of life tended to be idealized. The truth, as critics are coming to see clearly, is the very opposite. James himself knew well that he was a "mere stony, ugly monster of *Dis*sociation and Detachment" (*Letters*, 2:269). He seems to have been entirely serious when he said in 1898 (alluding to British and American imperialism), "Thank God, however, I've no *opinions*—not even on the Dreyfus case. I'm more and more only aware of things as a more or less mad panorama, phantasmagoria and dime museum" (*Letters*, 1:310–11). And although he could be passionate enough about some things, his advice to Vernon Lee remained a rule for him: "Morality is hot—but art is icy."

It is not surprising that he admired writers who did their utmost to avoid sentimentality and to cultivate a "scientific" impersonality. James's icy analysis of the aggressive and defensive strategies of human beings is inseparable from his conviction that the French naturalists, despite their excessive permissiveness, pessimism, and occasional unsavoriness, were writing the best fiction of the nineteenth century. His desire to achieve impersonality and detachment in his own work is equally reflected in his statement that he hoped to write in such a way that it would be impossible for the reader to know whether he was English or American. F. O. Matthiessen was unquestionably right when he said that James's novels "are the great monument in American fiction to the skills of detachment and observation."[6] In the end it is detachment that James worships—the detachment that frees men from the enslaving, warlike world.[7]

4
The Eye, Appearances, and Acting

"The only thing is that I have to act as it demands of me."
"To 'act'?" said Mrs. Assingham with an irrepressible quaver.
"Isn't it acting, my dear, to accept it? I do accept it."
—Henry James, *The Golden Bowl*

If all the world's a stage, Henry James knew that he was no active performer before the hot glare of the footlights. He could only envy the world's actors, those active performers who seemed to delight in showing themselves to others, in being conspicuous—in conspicuous waste and conspicuous display. As for himself, he shrank back, "fearing notice most," preferring to experience life indirectly—from the wings. So in *Notes of a Son and Brother* when he recounts his "exposure" in the "moot-court" of the Harvard Law School (of which he was "a singularly alien member") he views his ordeal in the imagery of the fierce glare of publicity and the terror of an actor who has lost his composure:

> . . . I have kept to this hour a black little memory of my having attempted to argue . . . under what seemed to me a perfect glare of publicity, the fierce light of a "moot-court," some case proposed to me by a fellow-student . . . to whom I was . . . to owe it that I figured my shame for years much in the image of my having stood forth before an audience with a fiddle and bow and trusted myself to rub them together desperately enough . . . to make some appearance of music. My music, I recall, before the look of the faces around me, quavered away into mere collapse and cessation, a void now engulfing memory itself, so that I liken it all to a merciful fall of the curtain on some actor stricken and stammering. The sense of the brief glare, as I have called the luckless exposure, revives

even on this hither side of the wide gulf of time; but I must have
outlived every witness. . . . [*Notes* . . . *Brother,* 340–41]

Before the glare of others' eyes, he is exposed in all his inadequacy
and helplessness. Students of James's life may remember a similar
"luckless exposure" in James's confrontation with the *Guy Domville* audience, an exposure that prompted him to seek solitude,
to flee to Lamb House, where he would not have to face the "fiery
furnace of people" (*Letters,* 1:243). To Edmund Gosse he writes
in 1896: "But I stay in solitude. I don't see a creature. That, too,
dreadful to relate, I like" (*Letters,* 1:248). And to Mrs. John L.
Gardner he says that he will get away from London "as quickly as
possible into the country—to a cot beside a rill, the address of
which no man knoweth" (*Letters,* 1:239). Thus, like Adam and
Maggie Verver, James retreated to the hush and serenity of a place
like Fawns—or like Longdon's old garden in *The Awkward Age.*
But if the retreat from the world of appearances is dramatized in
The Golden Bowl—if Adam and Maggie employ Charlotte and
Amerigo to "do the worldly" while father and daughter retire in a
quasi-incestuous perpetuation of their established relationship—
the solution to the problem is also dramatized: Maggie must become an actress on the stage of the world—a "leading lady,"
leading others to do what she wants. James (who early in life
became passionately devoted to the theater, who waged his great
campaign to win success as a playwright, and who, in developing
his later fiction, always heeded the dramatic example and his own
admonition "Dramatise! Dramatise!") saw a solution to the problems besetting the divided self in the determination to resist retirement from the world's stage and to act decisively in the glare
of appearances.

   To trace the prolific development of the symbolism connected with appearances and acting—and the closely related symbolism of the eye, the organ that seizes objects in the visible world
—is to appreciate once again, the completeness of James's work on
the figure in the carpet. The world of the eye, in which "appearances insisted and phenomena multiplied," is once again the cage
(19:160); to be "of" this world is to be an actor, a performer, a
member of the "circus," a mountebank. And the motif of seizure
is expanded enormously in the imagery and symbolism of the vain

appearances that take the eye—whether glass, crystal, mirrors, waxed or glazed or varnished or gilded surfaces. All the radiance of the phenomenal world is contrasted with the natural and with the invisible, the real, the *ding in sich*. In short, James's imagination is, in the last analysis, animated by philosophical distinctions which have been central in Western thought ever since Plato. If James's escape from "ideas" was virtually absolute, we cannot forget his mastery over ideas.

But why, we must ask, does this imagery of acting and appearances—together with the recurrent opposition of appearance and reality, art and nature—come to be worked so obsessively into James's fiction? The artistic causes are clear enough: we shall examine them presently. But before proceeding to that, we can deepen our understanding of James's art by inquiring into the psychic origins of his preoccupation with deceiving artifice, acting, and appearances. I would suggest that James's youthful experiences were such as to provoke anxieties that would tend to express themselves in an imagery of acting and appearances.

As we have seen, Leon Edel's biography establishes—conclusively, I should think—the importance of the sibling rivalry as a determinant of James's early conduct. So talented was William, so aggressive, so effective in dealing with the world, that there was, as Henry said, no question of his competing with his capable brother. What was left to him, then, but the effort to win the approval and esteem of his parents by some noncompetitive means? If he could not be superior, he could be good. He could be the loving, cooperative child, the child who caused no trouble whatsoever and who won his parents' love and esteem by his unparalleled goodness.

The data confirm that some such strategy was adopted by the young Henry. If he was, by his own testimony, obedient and docile, in contrast to the aggressive and active William, his father too takes special note of Henry's compliant nature in a letter written shortly before the father's death. This letter is as ominous, from a psychiatrist's point of view, as it is touching:

> And now, my darling boy, I must bid you farewell. How loving a farewell it is I can't say, but only that it is most loving. All my children have been very good and sweet from their infancy, and I have been very proud of you and Willy. But I can't help feeling

that you are the one that has cost us the least trouble, and given us always the most delight. Especially do I mind mother's perfect joy in you the last few months of her life, and your perfect sweetness to her. I think in fact it is this which endears you so much to me now.[1]

Again, we find the father writing to Henry: "Indeed, you are always in our hearts and thoughts, and mother, I think, loves you more than all her other progeny."[2] Small wonder that William dubbed his perfect and sweet brother with the satiric nickname "Angel." Nor is it surprising that the mother should become embrued about Henry's "dear reasonable over-conscientious soul" or that James's fiction might become concerned (as F. O. Matthiessen has noted) with the "multiplication of 'scruples' and 'considerations.' "[3]

But such conformity to his parents' wishes, such perfect sweetness and pliancy, prove costly. The good, docile, angelic Henry is not the whole Henry. To please others he must cease to assert himself, indeed must efface himself and "surrender" to the will of others. But such an absence of self-assertion comes precariously close to the absence of selfhood: it is as if the self were lost in the mask, the role, of docility. Moreover, to shrink from life, to take it "indirectly," is in a sense to desire an exceedingly dangerous peace and safety—the security of risking nothing and of being nothing in the world. The injury to James's back may well be connected with such a retreat from the battle of life. If he could not act positively, aggressively, he would be driven to find an excuse for his disinclination to involve himself in the world of action. Later in life he would see himself clearly and remorselessly as "that queer monster the artist," a man whose "loneliness" was a central fact of his being (*Letters*, 2:269). But in a young man only some physical incapacity could justify the queerness, the shrinking from action and aggression.

It seems fair to conclude, then, that in erecting a system of defenses against a threatening reality, James was to a degree constructing what R. D. Laing calls a "false-self system," a means of preventing others from seeing into the true and vulnerable self. We must therefore examine two closely related motifs dominating the consciousness of the individual who constructs a false self: first, the idea of acting; second, the fear of seizure by the eye.

In connection with the idea of acting, R. D. Laing describes one of his patients, a young man named David, whose "view of human nature in general, based on his own experience of himself, was that everyone was an actor." In his desperate effort to make himself secure, this young man developed a false self, for "by always playing a part he found he could in some measure overcome his shyness, self-consciousness, and vulnerability." "His ideal was, never to give himself away to others."[4] Since it is the false self that confronts and deals with the world, the real self is never threatened. And Laing sees in this attempt to face the world through an intermediary—in this removal of the true self from the threat of engulfment—an effort to gain perfect invulnerability, imperviousness, omnipotence. "The imagined advantages" of such a strategy "are safety for the true self, isolation and hence freedom from others, self-sufficiency, and control." Yet the shut-up or "encapsulated" self, being isolated, feels "more and more impoverished."[5] A sense of futility and impotence afflicts such a person, and he may contrast his own "inner emptiness, worthlessness, coldness, desolation, dryness, with the abundance, worth, warmth, companionship that he may yet believe to be elsewhere. . . . " Thus "there is evoked a welter of conflicting emotions, from a desperate *longing* and yearning for what others have and he lacks, to frantic *envy* and hatred of all that is theirs and not his. . . . " He feels that he is not alive and wants to "get inside life again, and get life inside himself."[6]

Laing's remarks on the role of fantasy in the organization of the schizoid personality, together with his analysis of the schizoid's "self-consciousness," can tell us a great deal about certain inveterate makers of fantasies—such as writers of fiction. The schizoid, in his isolation and detachment, cannot commit himself to a "creative relationship with the other" but is preoccupied "with the figures of phantasies, thought, memories, etc." Such a person is "omnipotent and free only in phantasy." The "unembodied self of the schizoid individual cannot really be married to anyone," Laing writes. "It exists in perpetual isolation." Nor does this unembodied self ever commit itself to action or to "the objective element" because "action is the dead end of possibility. It scleroses freedom." Laing concludes: "Without reference to the objective element [the self] can be all things to itself—it has unconditioned freedom, power, creativity. But its freedom and its omnipotence are exercised in a vacuum and its creativity is only the capacity to produce phantoms."[7] We have seen how the narrator of *The Sacred Fount*, building his "palace of thought," believes that he achieves such omnipotence. And Laing's remarks about *"envy and hatred"* have an obvious application to a writer who, from a psychiatrist's point of view, used his fiction to even a thousand scores with the active and worldly people whose "crude complacency of power" had crushed him, as a child, "to sadness" (*Small Boy*, p. 236).

The preoccupation with the threat of the eye arises in this way: Self-consciousness for such a person, Laing explains, is "apprehensive awareness of oneself as potentially exposed to danger by the simple fact of being visible to others." The schizoid "exists under the black sun, the evil eyes, of his own scrutiny," and he feels he has to be continually aware of himself to guarantee his "continued existence."[8] But because he is subject to the gaze of others, he is vulnerable. Laing writes:

> Awareness of an object lessens its potential danger. Consciousness is then a type of radar, a scanning mechanism. The object can be felt to be under control. As a death ray, consciousness has two main properties: its power to petrify (to turn to stone: to turn oneself or the other into things); and its power to penetrate. Thus, if it is in these terms that the gaze of others is experienced, there is a constant dread and resentment at being turned into someone else's thing, of being penetrated by him, and a sense of being in someone else's power and control. Freedom then consists in being inaccessible.[9]

As for the origins of the division within the self, Laing stresses that the "patient's life in his own interpersonal microcosmos" is "the kernel of any psychiatric clinical biography" and calls attention to the "almost total failure of the baby to achieve self-instinctual gratification, along with the mother's total failure to realize this," as a "recurrent theme" in "the early beginnings of the relation of mother to schizophrenic child."[10] Beyond this, Laing stresses the role of conformity, the development of the false-self system in early childhood.

> Referring back again to [Laing's young patient] David, his actions seem from the beginning of his life to have been in almost total

compliance and conformity with his parents' actual wishes and expectations, i.e. he was a perfect model child who was never a trouble. I have come to regard such an account of the earliest origins of behaviour as especially ominous, when the parents sense nothing amiss in it all, but on the contrary mention it with evident pride.[11]

Laing's analysis of the schizoid personality is based on his experience with extremely disturbed individuals. But it is important to reiterate that the anxieties described in Laing's work, and the strategies for coping with these anxieties, are not peculiar to the abnormal: they are shared, to a degree, by many imagina·tive men—who have concluded that "all the world's a stage." What I wish to point out, therefore, is simply that the circumstances of James's childhood would naturally have given rise to anxieties like those described above and that James's imagination was, of course, to use these anxieties extensively in developing the subject-matter, structure, and imagery of his fiction.

It is not surprising, then, that the motif of encaging appearances is richly developed even in James's early work. Imagery of the bright and fetching appearances that conceal the actual darkness and constitute, for the free spirit, an exquisite bait, a beautiful trap, is very deliberately developed, for example, in *The American*. At the beginning of the novel Newman is in the Louvre—that world of art and appearances—and the note of warning is sounded by Mr. Tristram:

> Ah, . . . you can never tell. They imitate, you know, so deucedly well. It's like the jewellers, with their false stones. Go into the Palais Royal there; you see "Imitation" on half the windows. The law obliges them to stick it on, you know; but you can't tell the things apart. [2:19]

Newman indeed has already been seduced by an appearance. Mlle. Noémie, the copyist, the imitator, presents the appearance of a diligent art student and a lady; but she is only acting a part:

> As the little copyist proceeded with her task, her attention addressed to her admirer, from time to time, for reciprocity, one of its blankest, though not briefest, missives. The working-out of her scheme appeared to call, in her view, for a great deal of vivid by-play, a great standing off with folded arms and head drooping

from side to side, stroking of a dimpled chin with a dimpled hand, sighing and frowning and patting the foot, fumbling in disordered tresses for wandering hair-pins. These motions were accompanied by a far-straying glance, which tripped up, occasionally, as it were, on the tall arrested gentleman. [*The American*, 2:5]

The young copyist has an "aptitude for playing a part at short notice" (2:6). She appears charming and proper, but in truth she is a grasping materialist (her chief interest is clothes) and a saleable commodity, as we later learn. For all her apparent youth and vitality, when Newman sees her after she has sold herself to a wealthy fifty-year-old man, Mlle. Noémie shows the "quiet" of those who have surrendered to the world:

> [Newman] observed the change in her appearance and that she was very elegant, really prettier than before; she looked a year or two older, and it was noticeable that, to the eye, she had only added a sharp accent to her appearance of "propriety," only taken a longer step toward distinction. She was dressed in quiet colours and wore her expensively unobstrusive gear with a grace that might have come from years of practice. Her presence of mind, her perfect equilibrium, struck Newman as portentous. . . . [2:291]

But if Noémie, the "perfect Parisienne," knows her appearances and acts a part with facility, there are those even more practiced in this wordly art. Thus when Newman threatens Madame de Bellegarde, and reveals that he possesses the note proving that she tried to kill her husband, the old woman is superb: " 'What paper is this you speak of?' asked the old lady, with an imitation of tranquility which would have been applauded in a veteran actress" (1877 edition, p. 431). And at Madame de Cintré's, Newman sits "looking at the entrances and exits" of her guests:

> He felt as if he were at the play and as if his own speaking would be an interruption; sometimes he wished he had a book to follow the dialogue; he half expected to see a woman in a white cap and pink ribbons come and offer him one for two francs. . . . [Claire de Cintré] was part of the play he was seeing acted, as much a part of it as her companions, but how she filled the stage and how she bore watching, not to say studying and throwing bouquets to! . . . it was what she was off the stage, as he might feel, that interested him most of all. [2:144, 145]

But as he finds himself in this world of actors, he is himself in danger of losing his spontaneity. After an "extremely solemn" dinner at the Bellegardes', Newman finds himself becoming "for the first time in his life . . . *not* himself; he measured his motions and counted his words; he had the sense of sitting in a boat that required inordinate trimming and that a wrong movement might cause to overturn" (2:220). Momentarily, Newman is in the position of Isabel Archer, allowing himself to be "directed" (as she is by Gilbert Osmond)—directed into the cage of convention, in which all the other actors crowd.

Newman resists the Old World imitations and appearances, but Isabel Archer is not so fortunate. Indeed, the central question raised by the action of *The Portrait of a Lady* is whether Isabel will act naturally and spontaneously or will become a mere appearance, a portrait. And when she arrives at Gardencourt—that "picture made real"—and is initiated into the world of appearances, the dangers of artifice are everywhere. Madame Merle, for example is "not natural," is a "charming surface"; and, as she says to Isabel, "a woman . . . has to remain on the surface and, more or less, to crawl" (*Portrait*, 3:274, 280). Osmond, living in the cold house of artifice—a house which "[composes] well"—is the man who is "artistic through and through" and whose face is "modelled and composed," "overdrawn, retouched" (3:325, 352, 376). When Isabel meets Osmond, she sits quietly, "as if she had been at the play," and at length she becomes, horrifyingly, the woman forced to live only for appearances, the portrait "framed in the gilded doorway, . . . the picture of a gracious lady" (4:105).

In every novel James wrote after 1883, the idea that people become mere appearances was to figure largely. Thus in *The Tragic Muse* James's characters (with the exception of Gabriel Nash) are all "finished" and fixed like paintings or precious objects. Voisin has a "hard polish, an inimitable surface, like some wonderful porcelain that costs more than you'd think" (7:370). The Dormer family are "finished creations . . . ranged there motionless, on their green bench, almost as much on exhibition as if they had been hung on a line" (7:4). Biddy Dormer is "an English picture" (7:30); Lady Agnes has a "face of a fine austere mould," and her skin has a "singular polish"—a bit like the "extreme finish" of Voisin (7:5, 365). Julia Dallow is "a composed picture" (7:264); Peter Sherringham looks "like a Titian" (7:49). Miriam Rooth looks "like the finished statue lifted from the ground to its pedestal" (7:335). Mr. Carteret, propped on a pillow, looks like "a figure in a clever composition or a 'story' " (8:161). And Mrs. Rooth's bent back and head make "the subject for a sketch" (8:305).

Because all of these creatures are mere appearances, James makes it clear in the choral speeches of Gabriel Nash that there is no one who is the real thing—no one who has not sacrificed his liberty and spontaneity for the sake of the vain appearance. As Nash observes, ". . . we've so befogged and befouled the whole question of liberty, of spontaneity, of good humour and inclination and enjoyment, that there's nothing that makes people stare so as to see one natural" (7:178). Indeed, society as constituted in the nineteenth century consists of nothing less than an assortment of "mountebanks": "the preponderance of the mountebank, the glory and renown, the personal favour, he enjoyed," says Nash, is "the main sign of the time" (7:150). He argues further that "the great current of the age, the adoration of the mime, was almost too strong for any individual; . . . it swept one along and dashed one against the rocks." And he singles out, as illustrations of the mountebank's practices, exhibitions appropriate both to the actor and to the politician: "performances" and "speeches" (7:150). The illustrations are well chosen. Miriam Rooth, the actress, admits that one has to be "strange" "to want to go and exhibit one's self to a loathsome crowd, on a platform, with trumpets and a big drum, for money—to parade one's body and one's soul" (7:162). And Peter Sherringham sees her as but "a female gymnast, a mountebank at higher wages" (7:190). Nick Dormer expresses a similar resentment against his falsity as a politician: "A man would blush to say to himself in the darkness of the night the things he stands up on a platform in the garish light of day to stuff into the ears of a multitude whose intelligence he pretends that he rates high" (7:103). Yet Nick is an excellent actor—"surprised at the airs he could play, and often . . . [he] found himself privately exclaiming that he had no idea he was such a mountebank" (7:262–63). As he complains:

> I've imperilled my immortal soul, or at least bemuddled my intelligence, by all the things I don't care for that I've tried to do, and

all the things I detest that I've tried to be, and all the things I
never can be that I've tried to look as if I were—all the appearances
and imitations, the pretences and hypocrisies in which I've steeped
myself to the eyes; and at the end of it (it serves me right!) my
reward is simply to learn that I'm still not half humbug enough!
[*Tragic Muse*, 8:9]

Still Nick is fond of representation—of representing the borough
of Harsh as well as representing life in his paintings. Like Peter
Sherringham, he might have said: "I'm fond of representation—
the representation of life: I like it better, I think, than the real
thing" (7:78).

All of them (except, of course, Nash) like appearances better
than the real thing. Peter Sherringham, though English and
thoroughly modern, cultivates "the mask of an alien, an Italian
or a Spaniard; of an alien in time even—one of the wonderful
ubiquitous diplomatic agents of the sixteenth century" (7:49).
He appears to be devoted to art, but he is really interested almost
exclusively in his own career; when he announces that he will "be
a minister next year and an ambassador before you know it,"
Miriam Rooth exclaims, "And they call *us* mountebanks!" (8:
215). Basil Dashwood presents the appearance of a gentleman—
"he carried this appearance . . . to a point that was almost a
negation of its spirit"—but he is only an unregenerate actor using
the role of the gentleman as "his mimetic capital" (7:337). Julia
Dallow is also an actress—a "leading woman"—and, as Nick
Dormer observes, "Her charming appearance is half the battle,"
half the reason for her effectiveness (7:241). Living for and by
appearances, Julia inevitably inspects herself frequently in the
mirror, just as Miriam Rooth attends to the image in her "*ar-
moire à glace*" (7:239, 228; 8:210). By the same token, both of
these women have their portraits painted by Nick: both become
"portraits of a lady."

The fear of being trapped by appearances is closely connected
with the fear of the eyes; and in most of his fiction James works
extensively with the imagery of prehensile eyes that seize, fix, or
take hold of their victim, with the idea that the person so pene-
trated is exposed or stripped. The aim of the unregenerate aggres-

sor is to strip his victim of all defenses and thus to render him impotent. So it occurs that in *The Portrait of a Lady* all of Caspar Goodwood's advances toward Isabel manifest what Peter James Conn has called "the tyranny of the eye." When Goodwood arrives in London, seeking to seize Isabel and put her into his American cage, he has eyes of "remarkable fixedness"; and, like Henrietta Stackpole (or Madame de Bellegarde or half a dozen other characters in James's early fiction), he invariably fixes people with these grasping organs (*Portrait*, 3:116–17). Thus we see him sitting "with his eyes fixed" on Isabel, eyes that seem "to shine through the vizard of a helmet" (3:217–18). He tells her, "I hate to lose sight of you!" and refers to his project of "keeping [her] in sight" (3:222–23). Isabel remonstrates: "It's . . . being out of your sight—that I like"; and again: "I should feel you were watching me, and I don't like that—I like my liberty too much" (3:227–28). Thus she wishes to flee from that paralyzing, penetrating gaze. Her encounter with Goodwood in London ends, in fact, in her symbolic flight into a dark apartment where she can make out "the masses of the furniture, the dim shining of the mirror and the looming of the big four-posted bed" (3:231). It is perfect safety and invulnerability that Isabel seeks, the quiet of a convent or a prison, or a return to the "office" of her childhood where the furniture was stored. She wants the "freedom" from exposure to Goodwood's aggression.

As James's fiction develops, the handling of the threat of the eye becomes more and more symbolic. He creates a world peopled with those lacking a moral sense, men who have only a visual sense—an eye for things, for the bright surfaces, the waxed floors, the polished veneers, the radiant crystal, the glass and the mirrors that reflect light to appease the appetite for glitter. They live, these aggressors, exclusively in the world of the eye, of the vain appearance. In *What Maisie Knew*, for example, James creates a wasteland in which the chief motive of the inhabitants is conspicuous display. A society addicted to appearances has produced as its most characteristic types the Faranges, Beale and Ida; both are felt to be "awfully good-looking" and both are obsessed with visual effects. Thus Ida, the mother, whom James describes as "the striking figured symbol" (11:xii) has, inevitably, enormous eyes (the better to see and seize things with)—"huge painted eyes . . .

like Japanese lanterns swung under festal arches"—and a face "like an illuminated garden" (11:143–44). She is as "distinct and public as a lamp set in a window," and she produces everywhere "a sense of having been seen often, the sense indeed of a kind of abuse of visibility" (11:211, 8). Because she lives for and by appearances Ida becomes, in that metaphor James so often employed, an "actress" whose behavior constitutes a "scene" and a "presentation" (11:142, 218).

France, as the home of the artist, that creature of the eye, was always to elicit for James the rich profusion of imagery relating to entrapment in appearances. In *What Maisie Knew*, as in most of James's other tales, France is a symbolic land, correlative of the attachment or enslavement to the visible, the vain appearance. It is a France of bright reds and pinks and yellows, of "bright air," "pink houses," "red-legged soldiers"; its cafés, with their "painted spaces" and "red plush benches," have "the added charm of a circus"; the books in the shops are "yellow and pink"; and "a gold Virgin" is to be seen from "the old rampart" in Boulogne (11:231, 324, 343, 348). Small wonder that Maisie, poor victim of the world of appearances, is almost fatally addicted to all the radiance. Crossing the Channel, Maisie feels that "her vocation [is] to see the world" (11:231). Seeing, "she adored and took possession." It is clear that she has good reason to be "afraid of herself," for encircled as she is by such radiant appearances and by the vain bright slaves who flourish in this Vanity Fair, Maisie is in danger of worshipping—indeed of becoming—the gold virgin, symbol of the corruption of purity in an invidious world.

The imagery of bright and fetching appearances in *What Maisie Knew* is not a fresh development in James's fiction. It is prominent as well in *The American*, where Newman's red guide book, Mrs. Bread's red ribbon, Madame de Bellegarde's crimson dress, the red satins and silks, and the imagery of gilded, polished things and of glass and mirrors all betoken the eye's appetite for vain appearances. "The 'things' are radiant," says James in the Preface to *The Spoils of Poynton*, "shedding afar, with a merciless monotony, all their light, exerting their ravage without remorse" (10:xiv–xv). So like the author of *The Great Gatsby*, James creates what Fitzgerald calls a "universe of ineffable gaudiness."

And James pays particular attention not only to light but also to the colors red and yellow. Thus Catherine Sloper, in *Washington Square,* who has a "secret passion for theatre," treats herself to "a red satin gown trimmed with gold fringe" because she wishes to enter the great gaudy world outside her father's house (*Washington Square,* p. 93). In *The Princess Casamassima,* pink, rose, red, and rosy images appear again and again as emblems of the deceiving appearances that entrap Hyacinth Robinson. There is "Rosy" Muniment, who presides like a queen in Audley Court and who "works" others for all she can get—including a pink dressing-gown. There is Lady Aurora, who may suggest the cheerful dawn but who turns out to be an "idle, bedizened trifler" wearing a pink-tipped plume. There are, in Captain Sholto's apartment, "dim rich curiosities . . . glinting in the light of [the] rose-coloured lamp" (5:265). When Hyacinth visits that consummate actress, the Princess Casamassima, he sinks into the "most sumptuous" chair, whose seat is "covered with rose-coloured brocade and of which the legs and frame appeared of pure gold" (5:284). Finally, there is an allusion to redness in Paris, where Hyacinth reflects that the French revolution was "a sunrise out of a sea of blood." In *The Princess Casamassima,* as in *The Ambassadors,* Paris is the city of light, "brilliant with illuminations, with the variety and gaiety of the crowd, the dazzle of shops and cafés seen through uncovered fronts or immense lucid plates, the flamboyant porches of theatres and the flashing lamps of carriages. . . ." (6:119).

Meanwhile, James continues to work everywhere with the imagery of acting. There is something "theatrical" about Hyacinth Robinson: "he was to go through life in a mask, in a borrowed mantle; he was to be every day and every hour an actor" (5:79, 86). He "masquerades" both in "high life" and in low (6:89). Lady Aurora suggests "a personage in a comedy" (5:123); Vetch suggests "the odour of stage-paint" (6:154); Sholto is "a masquerader" and "four-fifths" of his feelings are "purely theatrical" (5:250; 6:83). And it is in a box at the theatre that Hyacinth meets the Princess—a box that "framed the bright picture of the stage and made one's own situation seem a play within a play" (5:208). The Princess's designs on Hyacinth are associated with the "plot" of the play, and her performance of the part she has undertaken to play is "complete" (6:19). No one is what he seems in this novel—London is like Hamlet's Elsinore—and everywhere Hyacinth encounters "high, imposing shadows of objects low and mean" (6:110).

The same world of color, light, theatrical appearances, and prehensile eyes is developed with luxuriant detail in the novels of James's major phase. Consider the motif of showing in *The Wings of the Dove*. It is announced in the first sentence: Kate Croy "showed herself, in the glass over the mantel, a face positively pale. . . . " (19.3). Kate finds herself, even in the tarnished mirror in her father's shabby apartment, "agreeable to see"; and James observes that she is "somehow always in the line of the eye" (19:5). Thereafter, the word *shows* is employed everywhere to describe Kate's actions, with the unmistakable implication that she lives exclusively in the world of appearance.

When her father arrives, he too is all show. Kate reflects that "nothing could have better shown" what he is than his appearance (19:8). She judges his dress ("How he does dress!") and his "perfect look" ("You look lovely," she tells him) while at the same time "he judged . . . her own appearance" (19:8, 9). She finds it odd that there is "so much to show" in his apartment, but what shows, for her, is only the ugliness of it (19:12). Then Lionel Croy, seeking to get all he can from his daughter, tells her, "Show family feeling by seeing what I'm good for" (19:18). And at the end of the scene, when Kate asks him to assist her in making possible her marriage to Densher, Lionel "showed her . . . how vain her appeal remained" (19:24).

So Kate is forced into "the cage of the lioness," Mrs. Lowder —"a wonderful lioness for a show, an extraordinary figure in a cage or anywhere; majestic, magnificent, high-coloured, all brilliant gloss, perpetual satin, twinkling bugles and flashing gems, with a lustre of agate eyes, a sheen of raven hair, a polish of complexion. . . . " (19:30). It it here, at Lancaster Gate, where "appearances insisted and phenomena multiplied," where all things are "touches in a picture and denotements in a play," that Kate is "offered to the sight" of Milly Theale and appears as "a figure in a picture stepping by magic out of its frame" (19:160,

148, 146, 171). And yet Milly takes all of these appearances to be "real" (19:171). James plays ironically with the word "real" throughout *The Wings of the Dove*, while constantly making it clear that the reality which Milly confronts is entirely "show." Thus when Milly visits the National Gallery, she confuses a casual reference to Merton Densher ("Handsome? Well, if you choose to say so") with a reference to a picture (19:291). Like a painting, Densher exhibits "the English style"; and James implies that one can't, after all, distinguish the appearance of the man from the man himself (19:292).

As the conspiracy of Kate and Densher develops, both become actors. Kate has "to dress the part, to walk, to look, to speak, in every way to express, the part" of "the character she had undertaken, under her aunt's roof, to represent" (20:34). But she is, as we might expect, "a practised performer" (20:35). "Ah, leave appearances to me!" she tells Densher (20:49). The latter, however, is torn "between acting and not acting" (20:76). (James puns frequently on the verb *to act*.) Densher "could not accept the appearance of wondering how much he might show he knew [about Kate]" (20:85). Kate urges him on, however, and he passively submits to her direction. But when he sees Milly for the last time, he is scarcely able to endure his consciousness that he has put on "a brazen mask" and he virtually confesses his pretense (20:244). Milly disarms him, yet to the end he remains in Kate's power:

> "I'm in your power," Merton Densher returned.
> "In what way?"
> "In the way I show—and the way I've always shown. When have I shown . . . anything else?" [*Wings*, 20:401]

To the end Densher "shows" only his helplessness, his inability to free himself from the world of show.

As for Milly Theale, she is described by Susan Stringham early in the novel as "the real thing" (19:108). But the perfect freedom that she enjoys in the high Alps is meaningless unless it is tested in the world of appearances, and Milly must descend to "the labyrinth." Lord Mark advises her to "show herself" and to enjoy "the beautiful show" of life (20:151, 128). And Milly, heeding his advice, commences to "live." Refusing to show the terrible reality of her illness, she shows herself in Venice as a hostess, striking in her white gown and wearing the pearls that drag her "down to the ground." And finally she refuses to let Densher see that she knows the truth about his deceit. Thus, to the end, she accepts her role in the world of appearances so that, like Maggie Verver, she may "act" for love.

The theme of seizure by the world of show is orchestrated with even greater richness in *The Ambassadors;* but since I have already discussed elsewhere the associated motifs of acting, appearances, and the eye in that novel,[12] I shall confine myself here to a few brief observations. Central to *The Ambassadors* is the danger to Strether of encagement by "the vain appearance," by a glittering Paris, and by Madame de Vionnet and Chad. And we have observed that even Maria Gostrey—charming Maria!—takes hold of Strether with her eyes "as if he were human material they had already in some sort handled." For Waymarsh, as we have seen, Maria is associated with the dangers of Europe and the Catholic Church, which he views as "the enemy, the monster of bulging eyes and far-reaching quivering grouping tentacles" (*The Ambassadors*, 21:41). Those "bulging eyes" suggest the threat, once again, of the world of appearances; and it is small wonder that Maria's apartment, crowded with precious possessions, is a place where "the lust of the eyes and the pride of life had indeed thus their temple" (21:119). Moreover, as we might expect, the vivid colors that stimulate the lust of the eyes are everywhere in this city of the eye. There are the seventy volumes of Victor Hugo in "red and gold" that Strether purchases; there is the "crimson-and-gold elegance" of Sarah Pocock's hotel room; there is "the red velvet band" that Maria Gostrey wears "round her throat." Strether's surrender to Madame de Vionnet is "made good" over an "*omelette aux tomates*" and a "bottle of straw-colored Chablis" (22:13). And James explicitly defines his symbolism when he refers to the "rose of observation, constantly stronger for [Strether] as he felt, in scent and colour, and in which he could bury his nose even to wantonness" (22:173). The rose of observation mingles with the gold of acquisitiveness, and nothing is what it seems. Above all, there is the light of Paris—the "dear old light" that is ambiguously "dazzling but dusky" and "treacherous." And there is the luster of the sun-king, the man of the eye—

Gloriani, "a dazzling prodigy" who "with a personal lustre almost violent . . . shone in a constellation: all of which was more than enough to crown him, for his guest [Strether], with the light, with the romance, of glory" (21:196).

As James described it in a letter to Hugh Walpole, *The Ambassadors* is "a very *packed* production, with a good deal of one thing within another" *(Letters,* 2:245); and James would seem to have achieved the sort of density and richness that he was seeking through his handling of symbolic motifs. Yet in *The Golden Bowl* he manages, astonishingly, to make his vocabulary of appearances, acting, and the eye even more expressive than that of the earlier novel. The most apparently casual and trivial transactions of experience exhibit the terrible addiction to enslaving appearances. James's people never simply walk into a room: they show themselves in it or they present or exhibit themselves. They do not simply come together and converse; they face one another in the hard glare of the ferocious world, they face and are faced, they expose themselves and are exposed. Human conduct becomes a public appearance, a performance, an act, a way of showing or exposing surfaces and fronts and sides (usually polished)—never the interior, the real, the invisible. What is important, above all, for these actors and actresses, these bedizened circus performers in the great whirling ring, is that they see or recognize or notice in order that they may know how to proceed—how to act with maximum efficiency. For if they get knowledge in their heads (as D. H. Lawrence so often declared) they gain an advantage, gain power, gain dominion. So they are continally looking, their eyes always fixing, seeking to seize the object and hold it fast, or to seize the knowledge that will give an advantage in the struggle for survival.

The motif of sight-as-knowledge is introduced early in the novel, when Amerigo, puzzled by "the extraordinary American good faith," responds to Maggie's remark that Americans "see too much" by observing, " You see too much . . . when you don't . . . see too little" *(Golden Bowl,* 23:11). And shortly thereafter he defines clearly his role as a member of the world of appearances:

"I'm excellent, I really think, all round [he tells Fanny Assingham] —except that I'm stupid. I can do pretty well anything I see. But I've got to see it first. . . . I don't in the least mind its having to be shown me—in fact I like that better. Therefore it is that I want, that I shall always want, your eyes. Through them I wish to look—even at any risk of their showing me what I mayn't like. For then," he wound up, "I shall know. And of that I shall never be afraid." [23:30]

To see is to know is to be safe—in the world of appearances. And, we may add, it is to possess. When Amerigo sees Charlotte Stant in Chapter 2, James plays on all of these meanings: Amerigo "knows" Charlotte perfectly, as if she were an object his eyes have examined so often that they totally possess her. But if she is thus exposed and "known" by Amerigo ("she showed him everything"), she is hardly disturbed by her exposure; she is quite at home in the world of the eye—the world of publicity and harsh light, of intimidating "fronts" and surfaces. She "shows" herself to everyone as "brave and bright," a polished object presenting splendid surfaces for inspection. The world of appearances is her home, the stage for her great act. She lives exclusively in the corporeal world of Locke's five senses and Newton's particles of light—the bestial world of getting and selling, of hunting and being hunted, the phenomenal world of time and extension. Existing as huntress in "the hard glare of nature," she is, like Ida Farange or like Gloriani of *The Ambassadors,* a sort of monarch presiding over the social scene: she is "crowned . . . in light and colour and sound" as she stands among revellers who appear "rustling and shining, with sweep of train and glitter of star and clink of sword" (23:246).

Small wonder that Fanny Assingham, after the assault of all this "showing," remarks that Charlotte "visibly knows how to swim" or that, faced down by the dazzling impudence of Charlotte and Amerigo, Fanny feels the need for "a sheltering darkness where she could muffle herself"—a place to bury "her exposed face, a face too helplessly exposed" (23:270, 276). For although Fanny is herself "an actress" in whom "the sense of seeing [is] strong," the "merciless glare" of the appearances that Amerigo and Charlotte present is too intense (23:276). Fanny senses an ugliness in that glare which is unendurable—ugliness from which the eyes must be averted. And this motif of an evil too hideous to be faced, a truth too horrifying to be known, reflects, once again, James's acute sense of the threat of "penetration" by the aggressors who operate so easily in the world.

But we have already noted that in *The Golden Bowl*, as in both the other novels of James's major phase, the protagonist does not submit passively to the assault, but instead asserts his own will against that of the persecutors. And, as we might expect, this turning of the tables involves an ironic reversal of the sight-as-knowledge, appearance-*vs.*-reality symbolism. In the second half of *The Golden Bowl*, it is Maggie Verver who has a "grasp of appearances," gives attention to her clothes, and begins "acting" and "playing a part" (24:52, 13, 8, 11). She becomes, indeed, the "leading lady" on this great stage, leading others to do what she wants (24:208). She throws off her "divine blindness," sees through the golden mist and the silver tissue of decorum, and proceeds to blind others: she throws "dust" in Fanny's eyes; she "blinds" Adam to her intentions; and her vision becomes as acute as Charlotte's (23:402; 24:38).

At last Maggie sees, and "knows," everything—the last iota of evil. But she continues to act as if she sees and knows nothing. In the final scene she recognizes that Amerigo, professing he has acted in good faith, is only throwing dust in her eyes, only "acting" still:

> "If ever a man since the beginning of time acted in good faith—!" But he dropped it, offering it simply for that.
>
> For that then when it had had time somewhat to settle like some handful of gold-dust thrown into the air, for that then Maggie showed herself as deeply and strangely taking it. "I see." And she even wished this form to be as complete as she could make it. "I see." [24:350]

She does "see," but not what Amerigo thinks she sees. She has waited for him to emerge from "the gray medium" of his oscillation, she has waited "for the light" (24:281, 282). But the light of love has not entered him; he sees only the light of the world, not that of heaven. So she has to avert her eyes from "the full glare" of his moral inertia (24:295). At the very end, to prevent them all from being torn to pieces, she takes pains to keep the truth from peeping "out of their eyes" (24:362). And in the last paragraph of the novel she continues her acting, pretending a blindness to the truth and surrendering herself to Amerigo's lust, yielding thus to a desire which is "like a light or a darkness" (24:352). She asks Amerigo to affirm that Charlotte is "splendid" —that is, to affirm that he is capable of rising above mere egotism and selfishness and of joining her in a tribute to sympathy and understanding, if not to love. "That's our help, you see," she tries to explain to him. But Amerigo, sexually aroused at this point, replies: " ' "See?" I see nothing but *you*.' And the truth of it," James says ambiguously, "had with this force a moment so strangely lighted his eyes that as for pity and dread of them she buried her own in his breast" (24:368, 369). The "truth" is that all he is capable of seeing is the object of his sexual desire; he cannot "see" love or compassion. He is merely a thing, like the golden bowl. Maggie responds to his ardor, but to try to put love into that cracked thing one must indeed be "divinely blind." More than this: Maggie's seeking refuge from the light of Amerigo's grasping eyes is exactly what the divided self, threatened by the encaging world, must do if it is to endure the aggressive "other." Like Isabel Archer and Fleda Vetch and the caged telegrapher of "In the Cage," like Milly Theale, who turns her face to the wall, Maggie cannot confront directly the "hard glare of nature" and must blind herself to the appalling truth of egoistic aggression. To be "divine," to love, one must blind oneself to "nature red in tooth and claw."

5
The Cage

She had flapped her little wings as a symbol of desired flight,
not merely as a plea for a more gilded cage and an extra allow-
ance of lumps of sugar.
   —Henry James, *The Golden Bowl*

. . . the supervision, the subjection, the submission, the view as
of a cage in which he should circulate and a groove in which
he should slide. . . .
   —Henry James, "The Birthplace"

We saw in Chapter 1 that James's view of himself as a passive
onlooker, condemned to "the habit of observation" and the "indirect" taking of life, suffuses *A Small Boy and Others* and how it
was characteristic of James to remark that on a night of revelry,
when others were enjoying themselves, he couldn't "indeed have
moved much" and "must have kept intensely still in [his] corner,
all wondering and all fearing—fearing notice most" (*Small Boy*,
p. 43). His imagination was to dwell repeatedly on people who,
like himself, have been immobilized or kept "quiet" by life—from
the "little Polish boys" in "Daisy Miller," who are "held by the
hand" as they walk about in the garden of the "Trois Couronnes"
with their governesses (18:4), to the aged Longdon of *The Awkward Age*, sitting in "sustained immobility" in the garden of his
old house (9:535). But James's resentment of the confining, narrowing, stultifying pressures of propriety and conformity was to
stimulate him to examine limitation and confinement in *all* areas
of human experience; and, taking the hint from his father, who
had raged against all that "finites" the human soul, James came
to see that limitation and confinement are, in the last analysis,
the inevitable consequence of our material being—of our willing-

ness and obligation to do the world's work for the world's base purposes. Thus, as we have seen, James could say that the world is one vast cage—"a sphere the confines of which move on even as we ourselves move and which is always there, just beyond us, to twit us with the more it should have to show if we were a little more 'of' it" (*Notes . . . Brother*, pp. 89–90). The great round world is a great round cage, and all of James's characters, tempted to become "a little more 'of' it," are destined to find themselves imprisoned and immobilized within that cage.

The symbol of the cage is prolific in James's work: it breeds a hundred symbolic associates. As James's imagination broods upon its central subject, it discovers that to put a person into the cage of the world is to fix or place him; to paralyse or petrify him; to smother him; to keep him quiet, immobile, passive. The world tolerates no freedom; it grinds out its products with an immitigable and remorseless persistence; it favors the cliché, the type, the stamped-out coin. Moreover, as we have seen, in the struggle for survival people inevitably treat others as things—mere products or articles for use—and seek to place others in positions of immobility or passivity so as to block all threats of independent action. But James goes even further. If people may be treated as things to push or pull or handle, they may also be treated as values, quantities, treasures, or masses, and like *objets d'art* they may be collected as objects of price. Thus the imagery of petrifaction merges with that of finance and commerce, and we find James gradually working this rich vocabulary into virtually every paragraph of his novels.

He began working out these symbolic motifs even in his early fiction, where the contrast between freedom and enslavement, between "living" and the living-death of convention and propriety, is pervasively developed. Imagery of mobility and immobility is especially prominent in the early work. If Daisy Miller is all restlessness, motion, and energy, she is surrounded by a host of conventional, circumspect people who would prevent her from acting freely and spontaneously—people like the chilly Winterbourne, who is too stiff to dance, or like Winterbourne's aunt, who is "very quiet and very *comme il faut*" (18:28). If Catherine Sloper responds eagerly to the theater and purchases a red-and-gold gown for a dance, "the idea of a struggle with her father, of setting up her will against his own, was heavy on her soul, and it kept her quiet, as a great physical weight keeps us motionless" (*Washington Square*, p. 167). So she is condemned to genteel retirement in Washington Square, where "the ideal of quiet and of genteel refinement" prevails (p. 94). Again, if Claire de Cintré, awakened from her sleep by the mobile, fast-moving Newman, begins to go to dances, she is surrounded by "motionless" and "fixed" jailers, like Urbain, the "man of stone," or like Madame de Bellegarde, perpetually seated in a fixed position, her gaze, like her will, "fixed" (*The American*, 2:156, 182, 197, 335, 340). The Hôtel de Bellegarde is "very quiet," says Claire, "but that's exactly what we like" (2:116). By the same token, Mr. Tristram advises Newman to take rooms in a " 'fine' hotel"— "something small and quiet and superior" (2:23). And Claire retires finally to the convent of the Carmelite nuns, where "everyone was very quiet" (2:479)—an anticipation of the plight of a heroine like Tina Bordereau of "The Aspern Papers," who, living in the "negative" old palace in Venice, is "terribly quiet," has "no life," and, with her aunt, is "worse off than Carmelite nuns in their cell."[1]

It is clear that any form of subjugation to the world or to another's will—any suggestion of "surrender" or submission— may release the symbolism of quietude and all the associates of that symbolism, such as sitting, keeping one's hands folded, or being held fast, or fixed. Thus it occurs that when Newman sees a chance to make Valentin into a businessman, when Newman's imagination begins to "glow" with the idea of stamping out Valentin in his, Newman's, image, James has his hero say: "There's no reason why you shouldn't have [half a million dollars] if you'll mind what I tell you—I alone—and not fool around with other parties. . . . *Keep quiet* and I'll find something nice— I'll *fix* you all right" (2:345–46, emphasis mine). And when Mrs. Bread, who has accepted that "a servant [is] but a mysteriously projected machine," compromises her liberty by failing to speak out against the evil of Madame de Bellegarde, she tells Newman, "I kept quiet. Quiet I call it, yet it was a queer enough quietness. It . . . changed me altogether. . . . I held my tongue. . . . I was as still as a stopped clock" (2:458, 459). Again, when M. Nioche is compromised because he has accepted three hundred francs from his daughter Noémie, he becomes "as quiet as the grave" (2:295). It is hardly surprising, then, that Gardencourt, in *The Portrait of a Lady*, is a place where the light is "quiet" or that "the tread was muffled by the earth itself and in the thick mild air all friction dropped out of contact and all shrillness out of talk" (3:73). This "quiet" appeals to Isabel Archer, and when the Molyneux sisters appear—"round, quiet and contented"—Isabel reflects that it is "lovely to be so quiet and reasonable and satisfied" (3:104, 105). And although Isabel shrinks from Caspar Goodwood's aggression, she is also drawn to him as to a "clear and quiet harbour enclosed by a brave granite breakwater" (3: 323). By the same token, she admires without reservation the woman whose manner suggests "repose"—Madame Merle—and the man, Gilbert Osmond, who does "nothing" and is "nothing" except "very indolent" and "too deadly lazy" (3:281, 391, 427; 4:46–47, 57). And after her marriage to this passive leech, she becomes, with him, "quiet and . . . serious" (4:105), her smile becomes "fixed and mechanical," and serenity is "painted" on her face (4:142). Eventually, of course, Isabel recovers some of her freedom; but to the very end there are moments when she sits "in her corner, so motionless, so passive, simply with the sense of her being carried, so detached from hope and regret, that she recalled to herself one of those Etruscan figures couched upon the receptacle of their ashes" (4:391).

As we might expect, the symbolism of the cage is equally pervasive in these early novels. Claire de Cintré, at first immured in the Hôtel de Bellegarde, with its "closed windows" and its "dark, dusty, painted portal"—a house "stoutly guarded" and answering to Newman's "conception of a convent"—later goes to the Bellegardes' country home, Fleurières, a house "like a Chinese penitentiary," whose gate with its forbidding "bars" is described as "a 'mean' crevice" (2:59, 113, 406, 425). Ironically, the woman whose "range of expression" is "as delightfully vast as the wind-streaked, cloud-flecked distance on a Western prairie," winds up in the high-walled windowless convent of the Carmelite nuns in the Rue D'Enfer, where from behind "a large close iron screen" Newman sees her and the other nuns chanting their "dirge over their buried affections and over the vanity of earthly desires." Whether the walls are built by Old World aristocracies or by

Catholicism or by convention and propriety ("the wall of polite conversation" and the "citadel of the proprieties" [2:260]), they are always a grave threat to the free spirit. Claire de Cintré is but one of many figures in the early fiction who are locked up in the citadel of the proprieties. In *Confidence* Blanche Evers and Angela Vivian are both locked up by Mrs. Vivian, their chaperone, who, as "a Puritan grown worldly—a Bostonian relaxed," constitutes the double threat of Puritanism and worldliness to the free spirit. "I don't like being deposited, like a parcel," Angela bursts out in protest, "or being watched, like a curious animal. I am too fond of my liberty. . . . I shall assume that, metaphorically speaking, Mr. Wright, who, as you have intimated, is our earthly providence, has turned the key upon us. I am locked up. I shall not go out, except upon the balcony" (*Confidence*, pp. 73–74). There is Daisy Miller, confined by propriety; "stiff" Europeans join with stiff Americans to prevent her from venturing abroad freely. There is Catherine Sloper, shut up in the house on Washington Square. And there is Isabel Archer, shut up in the Palazzo Roccanera—"the house of darkness, the house of dumbness, the house of suffocation"—"a dungeon to poor Rosier's apprehensive mind" (*Portrait*, 4:196, 100).

Poor Isabel is from beginning to end surrounded by prisons. Released from the bolted office of her childhood, she is in danger of being drawn into the "vast cage" of Warburton's life—"the system in which he rather invidiously lived and moved" (3:153, 144); the danger is also suggested by the ambiguous name of Warburton's estate: Lockleigh. Or, as we have seen, she may be imprisoned by Caspar Goodwood—"enclosed by a brave granite breakwater" (3:323). The symbol of the cage appears everywhere. Ralph Touchett's house in Winchester Square is "a limited enclosure," a place where no "fête-champetre" can occur, and as Isabel and Ralph sit "in the enclosure" there are "rusty rails" surrounding them and the scene is "perfectly still" and "limited" (3:200–201, 204, 205). Madame Merle is "blanketed and bridled" and her talents are "enclosed" (4:39, 270). The windows of Osmond's house are "cross-barred." Pansy's hands are "locked before her," and the convent in which she is kept is "a well-appointed prison" (3:367; 4:374). When Osmond declares his love, Isabel feels "the sharpness of the pang that suggested to her somehow the slipping of a fine bolt—backward, forward, she couldn't have said which" (4:18).[2] And at length Ralph's warning—"You're going to be put into a cage"—proves true (4:65). The "infinite vista of a multiplied life" becomes for Isabel "a dark, narrow alley with a dead wall at the end"; she realizes that she has plunged "downward and earthward, into realms of restriction and depression where the sound of other lives, easier and freer, was heard as from above. . . . " (4:189). And although she rebels against Osmond's propriety and base subservience to the world, she returns to the prison, where she is destined to continue to beat her wings against the bars.

To surrender one's freedom to the world is to become, like Osmond, quiet, inert, utterly passive. It is indeed to cease to "live"—to become a mere thing or product, stamped out by convention, handled or passed about by others, like a letter or a parcel sent through the post office, like a coin or a medal, like a piece of furniture. Thus an abundant symbolism of petrifaction appears in James's fiction, a symbolism that may be traced again, from a psychologist's point of view, to the anxieties of the divided self. Here it will be useful to glance once more at the observations of R. D. Laing.

The divided self, according to Laing, has an overriding fear of being "depleted, exhausted, emptied, robbed, sucked dry"; he fears that he will case to "live" and will be "turned, from a live person, into a dead thing, into a stone, into a robot, an automaton, without personal autonomy of action, an *it* without subjectivity."[3] Moreover, the term "petrification," as used by Laing, designates not only the dread of being turned into stone but also the act whereby "one may attempt to turn someone else into stone, by 'petrifying' him, and, by extension, the act whereby one negates the other person's autonomy, ignores his feelings, regards him as a thing, kills the life in him. . . . One treats him not as a person, as a free agent, but as an it."[4] The technique is "universally used," Laing points out, as a means of dealing with a disturbing "other." The people who use it

> both tend to feel themselves as more or less depersonalized and tend to depersonalize others; they are constantly afraid of being depersonalized by others. The act of turning [the divided self] into a thing is, *for him*, actually petrifying. In the face of being

treated as an "it", his own subjectivity drains away from him like blood from the face. Basically he requires constant affirmation from others of his own existence as a person.[5]

Moreover, the divided self cannot experience others as free agents because to do that is to open himself to "the possibility of experiencing [himself] as an object of [another's] experience and thereby of feeling [his] own subjectivity drained away. [He] is threatened with the possibility of becoming no more than a thing in the world of the other, without any life for [himself], without any being for [himself]."[6]

This double aspect of petrifaction is an obsessive motif in James's fiction. The hero-victim is "got hold of" and treated like a thing: thus Isabel Archer, Claire de Cintré, Hyacinth Robinson, Fleda Vetch, and a host of divided selves whom I need not list again. But as we have seen, the strategy of this victim becomes, in the later novels, that of turning the tables—of getting hold of others and forcing them to do the free spirit's bidding. Others are thus turned into things. Moreover, these attacks and counterattacks acquire philosophical significance, for they are connected with the old problem of man's freedom; and James, especially in his later fiction, contemplates the possibility that man may be nothing more than a thing, a machine, a watch wound up and compelled to run in the great time-machine of the universe. Like the French naturalists, James keeps asking: Who is free? Aren't we all in some sense slaves, products, stamped-out coins? Isn't even the "free" spirit driven by necessity—condemned to his "freedom" and enslaved by it?

Once again, we find the imagery and symbolism of petrifaction developed even in the early fiction. In *The American,* for example, the denial of freedom and expansion is seen in the creation of a dozen characters who have been poured into the mold of "Europe" and turned out as mere puppets of the Old World. Claire de Cintré has been "sold" to the Count de Cintré and is (or seems) a "great white doll," a thing that gives Newman "the sense . . . of her having been fashioned and made flexible to certain exalted social needs"; thus she seems "rare and precious— a very expensive article, as he would have said." And Newman sees her as an "object" that he can admire "in all its complexity," while reserving the right to "examine its mechanism afterwards, at leisure" (2:165–66). Similarly, Noémie, the complete little Parisienne, who declares, "Everything I have is for sale," becomes "a very curious and ingenious piece of machinery" that Valentin likes to see "in operation." By the same token, Noémie's father, accepting without question the way of the Old World, becomes a "smoothly-rounded unit" in Parisian civilization (2:67). And Urbain becomes a "clock-image in papier-mâché" (2:308). Even the habitations of the sold and enslaved victims of Europe give signs of the process of mechancial reproduction on an assembly line: the house of the Tristrams is "one of those chalk-coloured façades which decorate with their pompous sameness the broad avenues distributed by Baron Haussmann over the neighbourhood of the Arc de Triomphe" (2:35).

The American thus anticipates the elaborate development of the motif of petrifaction in the whole body of James's fiction. By 1881 James's handling of the motif is even more deliberate. Gilbert Osmond is a copy stamped out by the invidious world: "he suggested, fine gold coin as he was, no stamp nor emblem of the common mintage that provides for general circulation; he was the elegant complicated medal struck off for a special occasion" (*Portrait*, 3:329). As a copy *du monde,* Osmond can only copy: and that is why we see him copying the portrait engraved on an antique coin. He has also turned his daughter, Pansy, into a mere copy: a "consummate piece" and a "Dresden-china doll" that Edmund Rosier wishes to add to his collection of *objets d'art.* "Formed and finished for her tiny place in the world," "impregnated with the idea of submission," Pansy is not really alive at all: she appears with "a kind of finish," her hands "locked before her" or "folded together"; she has been made into nothing—"like a sheet of blank paper" (4:90; 3: 401, 333, 337–38). And if Osmond has made Pansy into an object, he does no less with Isabel, whose intelligence is for him "a silver plate . . . that he might heap up with ripe fruits" and whose imagination he wishes to "tap . . . with his knuckle and made it ring" (4:79). So Isabel becomes, for a time, a portrait, without any of the freedom or spontaneity of nature.

The question "What do you want to do with her?" figures prominently in *The Portrait of a Lady* as in all of James's early novels. It is equally prominent in the novels of 1886, in which James gradually extends the symbolism of petrifaction, quietness, passivity, and the cage. Both *The Bostonians* and *The Princess Casamassima* reflect James's disillusionment with "liberal" reform and with "liberal" reformers. For in both, the ostensible proponents of freedom turn out to be nothing less than vicious enslavers. Thus in *The Bostonians* Olive Chancellor, the ascetic, old-maid suffragette, whose strident advocacy of freedom deeply appeals to the innocent Verena Tarrant, becomes Verena's jailer: while talking continually about women's liberation, Olive weaves a "web of authority, of dependence" around the girl, a web "as dense as a suit of golden mail" (p. 170). Verena becomes Olive's "precious inmate," "shut up in Miss Chancellor's strenuous parlor," from which the prospect is a "general, hard, cold void" (pp. 180, 178). And then, seeking to escape this cage, Verena is drawn into another. Basil Ransom, the reactionary Southerner, whose "bohemianism" is contrasted with Olive's renunciation and whose "primitive" masculinity is set against Olive's chilly feminism, tears Verena away from Olive's "too clinching, too terrible grasp" and bears her away to his apartment in New York—a "hole" in a "row of tenements," whose balconies have an "elaborate iron lattice-work, which gave them a repressive, cagelike appearance, and caused them slightly to resemble the little boxes for peeping unseen into the street, which are a feature of oriental towns" (*The Bostonians*, pp. 190–91). The vista here is "truncated" and there is an elevated railway nearby which, we learn, "darkened and smothered" the street with "that immeasurable spinal column and myriad clutching paws of an ante-diluvian monster" (p. 191). Poor Verena is caged at last in the Old World of oriental slavery, of "epicureanism," and of male tyranny.

More penetrating, however, and to most modern readers far more interesting, is the handling of the theme of encagement in *The Princess Casamassima*. In his Preface to Volume 11 of the New York edition, James makes clear that the germ of the novel was his interest in the plight of sensitive people, like the telegrapher of "In the Cage" and like Hyacinth Robinson—people who find themselves encaged by their penury, yet endowed with vivid imaginations. His mind had often turned, James says, on "the question of what it might 'mean' . . . for confined and cramped and yet considerably tutored young officials of either sex to be made so free, intellectually, of a range of experience otherwise quite closed to them. This wonderment, once the spark was kindled, became an amusement, or an obsession. . . . " (11:xix). In "In the Cage" James considers a girl whose "opportunity" is "very much smothered" and who lives "in framed and wired confinement, the life of a guinea-pig or a magpie" (11:367). In *Casamassima* his attention focuses on Hyacinth Robinson's entrapment in Lomax Place—and on a hundred subsequent entrapments throughout the action.

To make the symbol of the prison as vivid as possible, James took notes, in the manner of the French naturalists, on Millbank prison in London; and in the magnificent third chapter he represents Hyacinth's mother, the French prostitute, as dying in "the circular shafts of cells," where "dreadful figures, scarcely female, in hideous brown misfitting uniforms and perfect frights of hoods, were marching round in a circle" (*Casamassima*, 5:47, 46). Visiting the prison, Amanda Pynsent feels "immured . . . made sure of," and wonders "why a prison should have such an evil air if it was erected in the interest of justice and order" (5:42). It is this sort of contradiction that James examines throughout the novel. For the horrors of Millbank prison are but physical tokens of "the high human walls, the deep gulfs of tradition, the steep embankments of privilege and dense layers of stupidity fencing the 'likes' of [Hyacinth] off from social recognition" (5:170). Like the character Tarrou in Albert Camus's *La Peste*, James might have concluded that the basis of society is the prison.

Hyacinth's entrapment by the aristocrats is developed in the episodes in which he is brought together with the Princess. The latter's interest in social reform appears genuine, but Hyacinth soon begins to wonder "if he were not being practised on for some inconceivable end" and feels as if "he had fallen into a trap" (5:211–12). Captain Sholto, who procures Hyacinth for the Princess, is, as Paul Muniment describes him, "a deep-sea fisherman. . . . He throws his nets and hauls in the little fishes—the pretty little shining, wriggling fishes. They are all for *her*; she swallows 'em down" (5:258, 259). The Princess tells Hyacinth explicitly: "I'm determined to keep hold of you, simply for what you can show me" (5:39). And Hyacinth becomes her "slave," sitting perfectly "still," in "willing submission," in her drawing room: "Hyacinth kept . . . quite solemnly still, as with the fear that a wrong movement of any sort would break the charm" (5:284, 293; 6:28).

Thus aristocrats join with plebeians in using him. Millicent Henning, who wishes to improve her status, regards the young man as a valuable object—having "a stamp as sharp for her as that of a new coin and which also agreeably suggested value." "What *do* you think I want to do with him?" she protests; and she asserts that she can swallow him "at a single bite" (5:72, 77). Even Anastasius Vetch, apparently benevolent, joins in the sordid business of using Hyacinth. "I made him, I invented him!" Vetch cries (6:241), and he works steadily throughout the novel to prevent others from doing what they want with Hyacinth—for Vetch wants Hyacinth to support him in his old age. Again, the Princess's remark to Vetch, "Leave him to me—leave him to me," is echoed by Paul Muniment's remark to her: "You had better leave my dear friend to me" (6:252, 300). To Muniment, as to the others, Hyacinth is but "a fine little flute," an instrument he plays upon freely, as he plays "consummately" on everyone for his own selfish purposes. And all of the revolutionists—Muniment, Poupin, Schinkel, and the enigmatic Diedrich Hoffendahl—are exposed as seeking only personal advantages and as wishing only to use Hyacinth. Indeed, the revolution itself is "a wonderful, immeasurable trap," whose "invisible impalpable wires are everywhere, passing through everything, attaching themselves to objects in which one would never think of looking for them" (6:49). Hyacinth is caught in the trap when, on his visit to Hoffendahl ("the holy of holies"), he takes a vow of "blind obedience": "[Hoffendahl] made me see, he made me feel, he made me do, everything he wanted" (6:50). In the end, Hyacinth discovers not a liberating revolution but only a sordid world of contradictions, a world in which every fair appearance (even the apparent saintliness of Lady Aurora!) is defiled by an underlying egotism and predation. It is not merely the "selfish congested rich" whom Hyacinth sees as responsible for the "abominations" that flourish in society; it is, rather, the entire "terrestrial globe" —a "visible failure"—that produces "the cause as well as the effect" (6:267–68). Unable to find any cause or any person he can believe in, Hyacinth commits suicide; there is for him no other way out of the cage.

If all the world's a cage, one might suppose that art, at least, was for James a liberation. There is much evidence (as we shall see in Chapter 6) pointing to precisely that conclusion. But James was never so sanguine as to suppose that one could enjoy liberty without paying an immense price for the privilege; and the truth is that the artist's life, as he discovered and acknowledged with characteristic detachment, was in its own way as enslaving as that of the most besotted bourgeois. James's father had suggested as much. We remember that each of William's choices of a vocation constituted, from the father's point of view, a "surrender," and that when Henry began to write, his father suggested that writing too was narrowing. The father's "power of suggestion" was indeed immense. When James visited the French writers in Paris—those "besotted mandarins"—they seemed to him worn out by "the torment of style," having "the look of galley-slaves tied to a ball and chain, rather than of happy producers."[7] As for himself, he knew that he was, like Joyce, nailed "to the cross of his cruelfiction." The very practice of his art involved a sort of enslavement: he writes in 1899 to Mrs. Humphrey Ward that the artist's "perception of the interests of his subject grasps him as in a vise. . . . he must there choose and stick and be consistent—and that is the hard-and-fastness and the vise" (*Letters*, 1:326).

So it is not surprising that when James examined both art and politics in his novel of 1890, *The Tragic Muse*, he saw both as cages.[8] Both Miriam Rooth, the actress, and Peter Sherringham, the diplomat, surrender themselves utterly to careers that are represented, in imagery pervading the novel, as sovereign states and fanatical religions. And both characters are encaged. Miriam may resist Peter's attempt to "manage" her and to "lock her up for life under the pretence of doing her good" (8:340, 349); but Miriam's mentor, the old actress Madame Carré, is also a jailer and wishes to "keep" Miriam for the French stage (7:201). So at the end of the novel we see Miriam expressing the fear that even her triumph as an actress will shut her up in "a box" (8:397). Peter's fate is similar. He resists Miriam's efforts to make him give up his career and become her satellite; but in the end he finds himself "tied fast" to his ambition and "bowled about like a cricket-ball," "unable to answer for [his] freedom" (8:256, 287–88). As for Nick Dormer, he resists Julia Dallow's and Mr. Carteret's efforts to bribe him into the cage of politics. But after freeing himself from one cage, he finds himself in another: he is "shut up" in his studio and his devotion to art is a "trap" (8:300, 368). The motif of imprisonment is evident too in James's settings. Thus in describing the Théâtre Français, James develops the association between the prison and the convent that he had established more than a decade earlier. Miriam Rooth's visit to the *foyer des artistes* of the Théâtre is a pilgrimage to "the holy of holies"—to a place like "a church" or "a temple" (7:349, 354). But the note of warning against this religion of art is sounded in the description of the passage leading to the dressing room of the celebrated Voisin—a corridor having an aspect "monastic, like that of a row of solitary cells" (7:367). Voisin's room here is "an inner sanctuary"; and one is reminded of the "sanctuary" of Nick Dormer's studio, which is associated with "the monastery of Yuste" to which Emperor Charles V retired after giving up the throne (7:368; 8:274). As for the prison of politics, it is found in Mr. Carteret's mansion, Beauclere, an old brown abbey which, with its "red walls" and its "girdle of hedge-rows," suggests both enclosure and a temple (7:75, 84). Not surprisingly, we learn that Mr. Carteret wishes to "make sure of" Nick—to put Nick into the cage of liberal politics.

Equally pervasive in *The Tragic Muse* is the imagery of petrifaction. Both the artist and the politician become mere objects. Madame Carré, for example, is described as looking like "a thing infinitely worn and used, drawn and stretched to excess, with its elasticity overdone and its springs relaxed, yet religiously preserved and kept in repair, even as some valuable old timepiece" (7:117). Peter Sherringham, similarly, becomes "an expensive modern watch with a wonderful escapement." In the temporal world in which "success" is won, the successful become mechanisms, timepieces. And they do not hesitate to treat other people as objects or pieces of furniture—things to use and push about at will. As Peter says to Miriam Rooth, "You use us, you push us about, you break us up. We're your tables and chairs, the simple furniture of your life." Basil Dashwood, Miriam admits, is "like a lame chair that one has put into the corner" (7:360). Mrs. Gresham, Julia Dallow's secretary, states that she is "almost a part of the house, you know—I'm one of the chairs or tables" (7:257). Mrs. Lendon, who cares for Mr. Carteret when he is ill, has "an influence" which is "a good deal like that of some large occasional piece of furniture introduced on a contingency. She was one of the solid conveniences that a comfortable house would have, but you couldn't talk with a mahogany sofa or a folding screen" (8:152). And Mr. Carteret's Chayer, "the immemorial blank butler," is similarly associated with things: "the tea-cups, the knives and forks, the door-handles, the chair-backs" (7:285, 288).

The imagery of objects and mechanisms is predictably carried out in the descriptions of Miriam Rooth, Julia Dallow, and the actress Voisin. Miriam's face, like that of Madame Carré, is "an elastic substance, an element of gutta-percha, like the flexibility of the gymnast, the lady at the music-hall who is shot from the mouth of a cannon"; it becomes, indeed, "a finer instrument than old Madame Carré's" (7:190). Her body, Miriam says, is only "machinery"—machinery that one shows "for money"; and her talent is "a box of treasures," which opens when "the key [has] slipped in, [has] fitted, or her finger at last [has] touched the right spring" (8:352; 7:338). But if Miriam is a machine with delicate springs, so is Julia Dallow, whose "constitution," according to Mrs. Gresham, is "wonderful": "it's a wonderful constitution. . . . the surface so delicate, the action so easy, yet the frame of steel" (7:257). And Voisin, too, is "an object . . . an instrument for producing rare sounds, to be handled, like a legendary violin, with a recognition of its value"; she has a "hard polish, an inimitable surface, like some wonderful porcelain that costs more than you'd think" (7:366, 370).

The Tragic Muse has been described as James's "last Victorian novel,"[9] and it unquestionably marks a turning point in James's career. There is nothing essentially new in the imagery of the novels of the nineties and of his major phase, but after 1890 James was able to write a fiction in which virtually every paragraph carries symbolic significance; and his determination to work his symbolic motifs ever more densely into his prose is one major reason his style becomes "labored" and "congested." Consider,

for example, the remarkable proliferations of the motif of petrifaction into the imagery of finance and "quantities" in these later
novels.

In the early fiction James is content to associate his villains
with mathematics or quantities. In *Washington Square,* for example, we find Dr. Sloper (that perfect "man of the world")
asking, "Shall a geometrical proposition relent?" and Morris
Townsend reasoning that Dr. Sloper's opposition to his marriage
with Catherine is "the unknown quantity in the problem he had
to work out . . . but in mathematics there are many short cuts,
and Morris was not without a hope that he should discover one"
(pp. 200, 206). In *Confidence* Gordon Wright is seen making a
"chemical analysis—a geometrical survey—of the lady of his
love" (p. 19). In *The Bostonians* Basil Ransom is described as
having a face "a little hard and discouraging, like a column of
figures" (p. 4). And in *The Tragic Muse* Peter Sherringham regards Miriam Rooth as a "very important quantity," of which
"every inch" is "dear and delightful" (7:316; 8:257).

By the time James wrote *The Spoils of Poynton,* however, the
imagery of finance and quantification has multiplied so vigorously
that the words *profit, count, value, sum, accumulations, commerce, debt, gain,* and *reward* appear on virtually every page.
These words are far more than dead metaphors; they articulate
James's vision of life as a sordid bookkeeping conducted to gratify
the will to power and to "protract the profit" of immitigably selfish appetites. People, like the spoils themselves, may be "treasures" and we see James's collectors incessantly calculating the
value of their friends and acquaintances, their human acquisi-
tions; we see them reckoning, weighing, counting, estimating.
Fleda Vetch becomes a "bargain" and one of Mrs. Gereth's "best
finds." And if Mrs. Gereth may profit from Fleda's companionship, Fleda may profit as well from Mrs. Gereth's. It is true that
Fleda's father "never reproached her with profitable devotions;
so far as they existed he rather studied to glean from the same
supposed harvest." Still the rumor goes round that Fleda is "all
but paid in shillings" by Mrs. Gereth, from whom Fleda does
receive an "admirable dressing-bag" (*Spoils,* 10:61, 53). Moreover, Fleda may "profitably devote the moments" before she sees
Mrs. Gereth to considering that the marriage of Owen and Mona

can be shattered if Fleda reveals that Mona insists on getting the spoils; and Fleda can feel Owen's desire for her as "the rush of a flood into her own accumulations" or can look on the possibility of Mona's refusing Owen as a "calculation" affecting "the total of her sentiments" (10:105, 108). After her "commerce" with Mrs. Gereth, Fleda may feel that she is "in Mrs. Gereth's debt," but she can also reflect that "it shouldn't be for nothing that she had given so much; deep within her burned the resolve to get something back" (10:130, 134).

The imagery of finance and quantities extends to every feeling. Fleda's delight in her room at Ricks causes her to release "a rich sob"; and she is so ashamed of her pleasure that she feels she must "charge her emotion to the quickened sense of her friend's generosity"—not to avarice or her lust for the spoils. Again, she has a "rich fancy of how, if she were mistress of Poynton, a whole province, as an abode, should be assigned there to the great queen-mother" (10:146). When she flees to West Kensington, however, she is swept by "a horrible sense of privation": "she had neither a home nor an outlook—nothing in all the wide world but a feeling of suspense" (10:145). She has, in fact, only her "duty—her duty to Owen . . . but no sense of possession was attached to that, only a horrible sense of privation" (10:146). Again, the vocabulary of commerce fuses with that of moral obligation when she checks her books in this way: "She owed him something for her obvious failure—what she owed him was to receive him. If indeed she had known he would make this attempt [to see her] she might have been held to have gained nothing by her flight. Well, she had gained what she had gained—she had gained the interval" (10:182). She will try to "save what might remain of all she had given, probably for nothing" (10:195). But as compared with Mona Brigstock, Fleda is a poor financier. Mona can treat even her resentments "as if they had been poor relations who needn't put her to expense" (10:199). But Fleda, lacking such capital to draw upon, feels Mrs. Gereth's pressure upon her as "the presentation of a heavy bill before which Fleda could only fumble in a penniless pocket" (10:203). Thus Mrs. Gereth becomes master of the situation, waxes rich, speaks with "a rich humour," and has a "wealth . . . of certitude" (10:206).

The full, ironic truth of *The Spoils of Poynton*, then—the

truth that keeps arising in the symbolism of finance and reckoning—can only undercut any high pretensions to honor and a moral sense. Even the sublimest feelings may be "counted" or may constitute a "gain" or a "loss." In the material world, possession is all, and there are countless Fleda Vetches who, in the sacred solitude of their daydreams, imagine "rising" to become the beautiful keepers of the spoils, tokens of the one true religion, faith in "the things."

The imagery of finance and quantification becomes obsessive in these novels of the nineties—as we might have expected in a writer who perceived early in life that "mere brute quantity and number" are reserved for those who "go in for everything and every one." We remember how James envied children who had discovered the secrets of arithmetic that he was never quite able to divine; and how, as a child, he was cut off from all "questions of the counting-house and of the market" (*Small Boy*, pp. 290, 223, 189). Denied access to this worldly knowledge, he is fascinated by the impressment of youth—"helpless plasticity"—into the world of getting and spending. Both in *What Maisie Knew* and in *The Awkward Age* his young heroines, caged in the material world, are irredeemably sullied by it. As we have seen in our discussion of the divided self (Chapter 2), Nanda Brookenham surrenders to the sordid game of acquisition and contents herself with the safety and affluence provided by the aged Longdon. In much the same way, Maisie Farange, tutored throughout her early life by the vain acquisitive slaves of the world, learns that getting is one's primary obligation. She learns from Mrs. Beale, for example, "the idea of getting what one wanted: one got it . . . by 'making love' " (11:300); she learns from Sir Claude that bribery is the normal way of getting people to do what you want (11:263); she learns from Mrs. Wix that the basic relationship between people is that of the purchaser and the purchased: the Countess "pays" for Beale, Sir Claude "pays" for Mrs. Beale, and (Maisie completes the demonstration) Sir Claude pays for Mrs. Wix too (11:276–77). So Maisie is drawn inexorably to the idea of accumulating the spoils, and when she sits looking at the statue of the gold Virgin, the full ironic truth of her encagement in the material world is exposed with devastating clarity.

The most brilliant development of the symbolism of finance

and quantification, however, is to be found in James's last novels, where the rapacious counting and calculating of the acquisitive clerks in this great counting-house world becomes, blackly, a sort of reckoning of stones—human stones that coldly and efficiently reduce everything in life to quantitative terms. In *The Golden Bowl,* the idea of a mass or quantity or value to be measured arises everywhere. After the first scene, in which Amerigo stops before a window containing objects "massive and lumpish, in silver and gold," we discover that the entire world consists of nothing but such masses. Amerigo is one of "the smaller pieces," —"one of the little pieces that you unpack at hotels." (23:13, 14). And while Maggie believes that "the finest objects are often the smallest," she does not realize that her golden bowl is cracked and will become, as last, nothing but "worthless fragments." As for Maggie's own value, it is reduced because she has no "wealth of kinship," but then she has the Verver millions; and as an extra dividend, Amerigo reflects, she has "character"—so he feels "his accounts so balanced as they had never done in his life before" (23:3, 9, 14, 19).

But Amerigo's reduction of all human beings and experiences to cash and quantitative values is not unique: all of the clerks in James's great counting-house world are given to numerical reckoning. Fanny Assingham, for example, speaks of her faith in Amerigo "as she might have quoted from a slate, after adding up the sum of a column of figures." Her "old arithmetic" may have been "fallacious, but the new [settles] the question." Her husband is seen "measuring these results." Mrs. Assingham also calculates "the quantity" of Maggie's knowledge about Amerigo and Charlotte "as if it were between quarts and gallons" (23:75, 76, 77). Later we see her wondering how some people come to be "so inordinately valued, quoted, as they said in the stock-market, so high," though they may not "represent their price." She reflects that Amerigo is "a huge expense assuredly," especially because he expects "some sort of return for services rendered" (23:268). Her husband is exasperated by her way of "adding [her] figures up," but Fanny can extrapolate from the most meager data; and in her "need to profit" from his impression, she continues as far as his patience allows, "weighing his charge" with the utmost care that

Charlotte and Amerigo will "manage in their own way" (23:284, 285).

The turning of the tables in the second half of the novel involves, no less, a keen financial calculation and measurement. Maggie's calculations begin after the episode at Matcham, at the moment when she perceives that something has happened and appears, "by calculation," dressed for dinner. "It was a wonder how many things she had calculated in respect to this small incident [Amerigo's entrance into the drawing room]—a matter for the importance of which she had so quite indefinite a measure" (*Golden Bowl*, 24:11). "Nothing she had ever done would . . . so count for her" as her waiting for Amerigo in Portland Place; and the moments she remembers of that experience are "firm pearls on a string" that she can "count again and again" at her leisure (24:10, 11). Her growing awareness of the adulterers' complicity is thus a kind of wealth; and once her suspicions are awakened, she also envisions the "profit of her plan" of becoming active (24:52). She has not, to this point, put Amerigo "to the expense of sparing, doubting, fearing her," and although Amerigo's tactful noninterference with Maggie's attachment to Adam constitutes a debt that she owes him—a debt that has "mounted up . . . like a column of figures"—she sees now that he may be the one forced to pay (24:76, 81).

Little clues and bits of information add to her growing "mass" of "accumulations" (24:15, 14). Gradually, Maggie acquires a wealth of knowledge and is in a position to make her nearly cynical offer to Amerigo. She can say to him: "Look at the possibility that since I *am* different there may still be something in it for you. . . . Consider of course as you must . . . what price you may have to pay, whom you may have to pay, whom you may have to pay *with,* to set this advantage free; but take in at any rate that there *is* something for you" (24:187–88). So she can offer the money or quantity of herself as a bribe if Amerigo will give up his equity in Charlotte. But before Maggie can take the profit she seeks, she must also somehow make Charlotte feel secure, free her from anxiety; and the "price," the "sum of money" that "Maggie must pay" to do this is considerable. Indeed, Maggie is "the one . . . to pay all"; the "quantity of compensation" is the total renunciation of resentment and, what is more, the need to give up her father, to grovel and pretend to be a fool, even to praise Charlotte in the highest terms she can summon up—to praise her for being "great"—"great for the world that was before her" (24:245, 327, 365). For Charlotte is indeed a considerable "quantity" in the world of mass and extension.

For all these exertions, Maggie is eventually "paid in full." But when Amerigo stands before her in the last scene ("he might have been holding out the money-bag for her to come and take it"), she realizes that the "payment" she is getting comes "at the expense of Charlotte." Amerigo, having withdrawn the money of his desire from Charlotte, is now ready to invest in Maggie. But "if *that* was her proper payment," Maggie reflects, "she would go without money" (24:368). If it is only a case of transferring his money, his sexuality, from one account to another, if he has not learned how to love and cannot understand or commiserate with Charlotte in her suffering, if he has no imagination of "the states of others" but is only shut up in the prison of his egotism, he is indeed a poor bargain—as flawed and worthless as the golden bowl. And all her efforts to redeem him have perhaps come to nothing.

So much, then, for James's most perfect renderings of the imagery of finance and quantities. The development, in these last novels, of the symbolism of the cage, of immobilization, of petrifaction, and of passivity, is equally expressive. And at the risk of repetition, we must glance at some of the most significant proliferations.

Consider, for example, the extensions of the imagery of petrifaction and passivity. The Jamesian world teems with passive, petrified people in the works of his major phase. There is Lionel Croy in *The Wings of the Dove*—a "product" and a "type," a man who protests that he can "do nothing" and is "like nothing" (19:8, 13, 20). There is Merton Densher, the man whose business it is "to keep thoroughly still," who has "nothing to do but wait" (20:264, 301). There is Madame de Vionnet in *The Ambassadors*, "beautifully passive under the spell of transmission," the woman who has "only received, accepted and been quiet," who sits with hands "clasped in her lap" and does not "shift her posture by an inch" (21:245, 247). There is Jeanne de Vionnet, the reincarnation of Pansy Osmond, the girl who appears with her "hands clasped together as if in some small learnt prayer" and who resembles "a picture"—"the portrait of a small old-time princess of whom nothing was known but that she had died young" (21:222, 259). There is Mrs. Newsome, who refuses to "budge an inch"—the "whole moral and intellectual being or block" that Sarah Pocock brings over for Strether to "take or leave" (22:368, 239). There is Waymarsh, the eternally Sitting Bull. There is Chad, "put into a firm mould and turned successfully out" (21:152). And there is Gloriani with his "medal-like Italian face."

Or consider James's rich elaborations of the imagery of the cage, together with such symbolic associates as chains, collars, straps, girdles, walls, bridles, cases, boxes, molds. In *The Ambassadors* Strether, released from the "prison-house" of Woollett and arriving in Europe with "such a consciousness of personal freedom as he hadn't known for years," encounters immediately the hotel-receptionist, "the lady in the glass cage" (21:4, 7); then walks off with Maria Gostrey, whom, as we have seen, Waymarsh associates with Europe, feudalism, and Catholicism (with its "far-reaching quivering groping tentacles" [21:41]). In Chester, Strether is backed up against the "rampart" of a "tortuous wall"; and Maria Gostrey puts to him her ambiguous question: "*Will* you give yourself up?" But Strether is also engaged in the sordid business of trapping and immobilizing others. Strether's mission is to provide for Chad "the general safety of being anchored by a strong chain" and thus "protected . . . from life" (21:71). Having passively surrendered to Mrs. Newsome, Strether intends to make Chad surrender too. The chain-image reappears when we find that Waymarsh is also taking orders from the American queen: "[Mrs. Newsome's intention] had reached Waymarsh from Sarah, but it had reached Sarah from her mother, and there was no break in the chain by which it had reached *him* [Strether]" (22:189). Again, the image bobs up when we see Miss Barrace, the complete Parisian, focusing Strether "with her clink of chains" and exulting that Sarah is "bricked up . . . buried alive!" (22:177). The image of the cage appears again in a reference to Sarah Pocock, who is associated (like Mrs. Lowder of *The Wings of the Dove*) with a lion in its cage (*The Ambassadors*, 22:80, 87). Images of collars pop up when we see Madame de Vionnet wearing round her neck a collar of "large old emeralds" and Maria Gostrey wearing "a broad velvet band with an antique jewel." Waymarsh is "strapped down," "cabined and confined"; even the girls whom Strether sees in Paris appear "with the buckled strap of oblong boxes" (22:57, 21:79). Finally, all of these images are gathered up in Strether's choral speech in which, glancing both at Woollett and at Paris, he describes life as "a tin mold, either fluted and embossed, with ornamental excrescences, or else smooth and dreadfully plain, into which a helpless jelly, one's consciousness, is poured—so that one 'takes' the form, as the great cook says, and is more or less compactly held by it: one lives in fine as one can. Still, one has the illusion of freedom. . . . " (21:218). It is in the struggle to free himself from the smooth and dreadfully plain mold of Woollett, and to avoid the stamp of the fluted and embossed mold of Paris, that Strether's ambassadorship acquires its singular poignancy.

Consider too the symbolism of the cage and immobilization in *The Wings of the Dove*. Both external "conditions" and inner "necessities" constitute the "great trap of life" in this novel. At the beginning of the book, Kate Croy's father and sister make it clear that they count on Kate to "work" the rich Mrs. Lowder, Kate's aunt, for all that can be gained; and Kate's loyalty to her family forces her into a "general surrender of everything." When Kate finds herself in Mrs. Lowder's hands—in "the cage of the lioness," the "counting-house," "battlefield," and "scene . . . of action" for this "Britannia of the Market Place" (19:30, 31)—she is like Fleda Vetch confronting Mrs. Gereth. She feels she may be "devoured"; and she can only play a waiting game in the hope that her opportunities to act freely will improve. But if she and Densher are rendered helpless by their need for money, Milly Theale, too, is locked up in the prison of wealth. "A caged Byzantine," Milly cannot "get away from her wealth" (19:256, 121). Like all of the world's automatons, she finds herself in "a current determined . . . by others" and "moving a good deal by a momentum that had begun far back"—the momentum of time, of history, and of the phenomenal world (19:274, 218). As Hawthorne in *The Marble Faun* had seen a Rome in which the past of sin and remorse is heaped upon the present, preventing all spontaneous enjoyment in the here-and-now, James here works with the idea that all the members of society are the mere products of the past and of the world. Milly's acts are "a chapter of history"; and as "heiress of all the ages," placed in the Palazzo Leporelli, which holds "its history still in its great lap, even like a painted idol, a solemn puppet hung about with decorations," Milly moves "slowly to and fro as the priestess of the worship" (*Wings*, 19: 118; 20:135). Small wonder that James describes the past as a "vast prison-yard" (*The Sense of the Past*, 26:48).

Like Strether, Milly struggles however to free herself from the past; and when she sees the poor of London, her "comrades," all locked up in "the same box"—the box of their anxiety about "the practical question of life"—she decides upon her "great adventure." Leaving her isolation as caged Byzantine, throwing off her passivity, she tries to "live." She may be confined in her fortress-like palace, but it is a "caged freedom" that she endures. And when, heroically fighting her illness, she leaves her room and comes downstairs to act as hostess—dressed in white and wearing pearls, "the long, priceless chain, wound twice round her neck," a chain that hangs "heavy and pure" and that suits her "down to the ground"—it is clear that she has chosen her enchainment to the material earth as the noblest expression of her freedom (*Wings*, 20:167, 217, 218). So she "supersedes" Kate Croy; and Densher, pierced by love for Milly, "something . . . too beautiful and too sacred to describe," is strangely altered—unfitted for his exclusive and passive surrender to the world (20:343).

Like *The Ambassadors*, *The Wings of the Dove* extends the symbolism of encagement in several new ways. One form of the cage is the circus ring. As we might expect, Mrs. Lowder is "the principal lady at the circus" who " drives round the ring," while Milly Theale is watched "as some spectator in an old-time circus might have watched the oddity of a Christian maiden, in the arena, mildly, caressingly, martyred" by "domestic animals" (19: 62; 20:42). Another form of the cage is the web—here the "wondrous silken web" in which Densher and Milly find themselves as "victims" (20:63). Again, James suggests the "crystal cage" of *The Sacred Fount* when he refers in *The Wings of the Dove* to the social "immersion" of the worldlings in Venice—"all together . . . like fishes in a crystal pool" (20:213). And there are scores of other passages in which James embroiders the motifs of passivity, surrender, and immobilization.

We turn finally, then, to the novel in which James's articulation of the imagery of encagement, immobilization, petrifaction, and passivity reaches its "rarest perfection": *The Golden Bowl*. An exhaustive examination of all these motifs in so complex a work would require far more space than we can reasonably afford to give in a single chapter, and such an examination would scarcely prove rewarding. But because the conflict between "active" and "passive" people is so essential a part of James's vision of life and because *The Golden Bowl* is unquestionably James's most searching examination of the problems inherent in that conflict, we can significantly extend our understanding of "the figure in the carpet" of James's entire *oeuvre* by looking carefully at one cluster of images and epithets relating to his lifelong preoccupation with the search for perfect safety and invulnerability in a warlike world. For what we find, when we look closely, is James's development of an idea central to Western thought since Plato's time: the conception of evil as the absence of being—as a sort of nothingness, as perfect passivity, utter inactivity.[10] In short, we find in *The Golden Bowl* the most comprehensive expression of the morality that informs all of James's work and that was present even in his earliest works.

To be passive, to surrender to the world as it is, to allow oneself to be caged or trapped—this is the overwhelming evil in James's fiction. But there is a radical paradox in James's working out of the idea. The most "active" people are, in truth, the most passive. People like Charlotte Stant may do and do, but for all their ferocious energy, they remain essentially inert and fixed; for they "do" only within the world of necessity, the enslaved world of time and extension. They never act spontaneously: they are always being driven—with all the pounding passivity of machinery. They are all "puppets pulled by strings" (as poor Fleda Vetch, to her dismay, discovers). Time and the material world pull the wires and they hop about furiously. But they are not alive at all; they are merely things, and they are neither free nor good. The pattern is announced early in *The Golden Bowl* when the key terms—*refuge, safety, peace, security,* and *passivity*—are set down like foundation-stones for the massive architecture to come. In the first scene Amerigo pays a visit to the Assinghams in Cadogan Place—the "final refuge, the place of peace for a world-worn couple, to which [Fanny] had lately retired with 'Bob' " (23:28). The worldly Fanny is like "a creature formed by hammocks and divans, fed upon sherbets and waited upon by slaves. She looked as if her most active effort might be to take up, as she lay back, her mandolin, or to share a sugared fruit with a pet gazelle" (23:34). She is, in fact, but "the *doyenne* . . . of her transplanted tribe" and has "accepted resignedly" her condition as Bob's wife (23:36). As for "Bob," he too has accepted resignedly. There is some question, in fact, whether he has ever acted independently. At least he did not actively marry Fanny: "I was your own," he tells her, "from the moment I didn't object" (23:86). He has allowed Fanny to determine his destiny. Moreover, as he says, he "disengaged, he would be damned if he didn't[,] . . . his responsibility" (23:64). He will have nothing to do with Amerigo's problem, and like a little child he takes refuge in *"his* box of toy soldiers, his military game" (23:64).

The conversation in Cadogan Place plays on the theme of passivity. Amerigo has been "conducted . . . to rest" in the port of the Golden Isles and is determined that his repose will be undisturbed (23:27). He is indeed so inert, so absolutely one of Adam Verver's possessions, that James repeatedly refers to him as a piece of furniture or a handsome building. He resembles a "Roman palace" with its "historic front"; or he is identified with the golden bowl, taken to be a "perfect crystal" and, because of his family's fall from fortune, like a "large goblet diminished . . . by half its original height" (23:113). Not that he minds. He is careful to ascertain that Charlotte's entrance on the scene will not disturb his tranquility. He sees that he is "safe" ("he had required to be safe") and that he need not bestir himself ("he was where he could stay" [23:59, 62]).

As we follow Amerigo through the succeeding chapters, we see him again and again refraining from action. Charlotte guides him and "he let himself accordingly be guided" (23:95). He shows total "inability in any matter in which he was concerned, to conclude" (23:11). As Maggie observes: " . . . Amerigo does not mind. He doesn't care, I mean, what we do. . . . Fanny . . . thinks he's magnificent. Magnificent, I mean, for taking everything as it is, for accepting the 'social limitations' of our life, for not missing what we don't give him" (23:175). And Adam Verver, when he decides to marry Charlotte, counts upon precisely this sort of "magnificence," declaring: "he'll just have to accept from us whatever his wife accepts; and accept it . . . just because she does. That . . . will have to do for him" (23:232).

But such acceptance and holding oneself "quiet" can pay dividends. Presently we see Amerigo and Charlotte rejoicing in the fact that to gather in the spoils of their lust, they have only to keep still. As Charlotte says:

> "Isn't the immense, the really quite matchless beauty of our position that we have to 'do' nothing in life at all? . . . There has been plenty of 'doing,' and there will doubtless be plenty still; but it's all theirs, every inch of it; it's all a matter of what they've *done* to us." And she showed how the question had therefore been only of their taking everything as everything came, and all as quietly as might be. Nothing stranger surely had ever happened to a conscientious, a well-meaning, a perfectly passive pair. . . . [*Golden Bowl*, 23:289]

The great ugliness of Amerigo's passivity is revealed sharply in the scene in which Charlotte comes to him in Portland Place, and he stands "motionless" waiting for *her* to act. He decides that he "would do nothing. . . . he would let her visit to him be all of her choosing. And his view of a reason for leaving her free was the more remarkable that, though taking no step, he yet intensely hoped" (23:295–96). Like some of those who passively watched the Gestapo bear off the Jews of Europe, Amerigo sees that he can profit from his very inertia. So he stands with "his hands in his pockets," a token of passivity that James repeats three times in this chapter (23:300, 302, 308). His "courage," as Charlotte points out, is "passive then—not active": the courage to wait for the pearl to fall into his lap (23:302).

Charlotte, meantime, is always the huntress, and her remarkable energy in the service of her lust reminds one of Kate Croy. But for all her eruptions of energy, she remains passive in the sense that she surrenders utterly to the world's conditions—she is incapable of rising above desire. "Haven't we therefore to take things as we find them?" she asks. "What else can we do, what in all the world else?" (23:303). In all the world, there is nothing else to do; it is only when the world is resisted that an alternative presents itself. Charlotte, however, remains, like Amerigo, a mere object that Adam gets to "make use of." She is like a cabinet or an intricate machine, with its "special beauty of movement and line when she turned her back, and the perfect working of all her main attachments, that of some wonderful finished instrument, something intently made for exhibition, for a prize" (23:47). There is obviously much "to be done with" such a fine object. Being precious, having "a value which is really inestimable," it "mustn't be wasted" (23:41, 291). Like Amerigo, she attests to "a rare power of purchase" and is at least equal in value to the "set of oriental tiles" that Adam purchases from Mr. Gutermann-Seuss of Brighton (23:196–97).

With a joyful fatalism, Amerigo and Charlotte accept their "placed" condition and at the first convenient opportunity make love. The "violence" of their embrace is stressed. Yet it is a violence tantamount to utter moral inertia, and it is precisely this quality that James stresses in describing their kiss: "Their lips sought their lips, their pressure their response and their response their pressure; with a violence that had sighed itself the next moment to *the longest and deepest of stillnesses* they passionately sealed their pledge" (23:312; emphasis mine). They are plunged into "the deepest of stillnesses"—a limbo of moral indifference and irresponsibility.

The turning of the tables involves inevitably an inversion of the symbolism: Maggie is transformed from passivity to activity and thus to "freedom." From the very beginning Maggie and her father have joined in accepting and perpetuating their established way of life. When they meet at Fawns, that temple of indolence which is "out of the world," for their "quiet hour of reunion," they seek out "one of the quietest places," a bench that is "sequestered"; "a pleasant hush" falls on them in their "serenity," and they seem to exhale into the evening air "a kind of helplessness in their felicity" (23:211, 155, 159, 167). They too, we learn, are like things. Adam's mind, suggesting the workings of a steel mill, is "one with the perfection of machinery," and there is "a spring connected . . . with the action of his eyes" (23:128, 131). Like Amerigo, Adam is no more than a building, "a small decent room" that presents a "side for the observer to study" (23:170, 157). And Maggie, like Charlotte, is an expensive object that may be "passed about . . . like a dressed doll" or, like a room, may be "furnished forth" or handled, with her father, like "labelled boxes" (24:51, 152, 69).

But if Maggie has been handled like a thing, we observe, at Fawns, the first stirrings of her desire for freedom. She is aware that there is no "life" in the seclusion of Fawns and that their peace is propped by gold. "The thing is," she tells Adams, "that I don't think we lead, as regards other people, any life at all. We don't at any rate, it seems to me, lead half the life we might" (23:175). They are "as free as air," Maggie remarks, but such freedom is "great" only "if we act on it. Not if we don't" (23:177). At this point, however, Maggie makes a grave mistake: instead of choosing to act for herself, she suggests that they "get" Charlotte Stant, who is "great in life," to stir them up. She is impelled, it would seem, by the highest motives: she wishes to relieve her father of the burden of fighting off women like Mrs. Rance. "It has to be too much of a fight," Maggie tells him; and because by her marriage he has lost his perfect safety—"the happiness of being just as you were"—she must do what she can to make it up to him (23:173).

The grave mistake—or sin—is, quite simply, her desire to ensure Adam's perfect tranquility: to make it unnecessary for him to struggle for anything at all. But to keep Adam "still" is doubly pernicious: first, it reflects Maggie's selfish desire to keep hold of him even after her marriage, when she has "lost [her] position"; second, it condemns Adam to inertia. By making "anxiety her stupid little idol," Maggie blinds herself to the necessity for Adam's moral exertion—the necessity of every man to "take his risk and lead his life" in opposition to the horror of "evil seated, all at its ease" (24:260, 81, 237).

Adam makes the same mistake. Instead of urging Maggie to bestir herself, he tries to "put her at peace" (23:223). He marries

Charlotte to assure Maggie that she need feel no anxiety about him: he marries "for [Maggie's] security" (23:225). But in seeking to "liberate [her] so far as possible from caring what became of him," Adam, in effect, enslaves her (24:81). And in the process he does not hesitate to enslave Amerigo and Charlotte, forcing Amerigo to "accept" his, Adam's, marriage and insisting that Charlotte "abide by what Maggie says"—thus keeping Charlotte, too, "at peace" (23:226, 237).

Once they have secured Charlotte to "do the 'worldly' for them," Adam and Maggie lapse again into their "pleasant ease" (23:318). But Maggie soon begins to see the fatal error of being passive: "What if I've accepted too passively the funny form of our life?" she asks herself (24:25). Amerigo and Charlotte, she sees, are doing all the "pulling" of the family coach, while "she and her father were not so much as pushing" (24:23). Adam, "so perpetually seated and so contentedly occupied," is apparently not awake to the danger (24:34), but Maggie's awakening comes in a rush.

James employs the symbolism of motion and exertion—of dancing, flying, lifting, and shouldering—to underscore Maggie's entrance into active moral combat. She has been like "a little dancing-girl at rest, ever so light of movement but most often panting gently, even a shade compunctiously, on a bench" and suggesting the "rather neutral and negative propriety that made up . . . the average of wifehood and motherhood" (23:322). But, rebelling now against her "placed condition," she decides that she will "go to balls again" (24:8). The "sense of action, . . . action quite positively for the first time in her life," now "kept her up, made her rise higher" (24:33). She is finished with sitting on benches: "she was dancing up and down beneath her propriety, with the thought that she had at least begun something. . . ." (24:51). She is like "some panting dancer of a difficult step" (24:222). Indeed, she begins to fly, to beat her arms in the destructive element: "action began to hover like some lighter and larger but easier form, excited by its very power to keep above ground. It would be free, it would be independent, it would go in—wouldn't it?—for some prodigious and superior adventure of its own" (24:186). She becomes thus "the overworked little trapezist girl" whom Fanny Assingham watches from the ground (24:302).

Even Adam, forever inscrutable, senses at last the need for action. As he confesses to Maggie:

> There seems a kind of charm, doesn't there? on our life—and quite as if just lately it had got itself somehow renewed, had waked up refreshed. A kind of wicked selfish prosperity perhaps, as if we had grabbed everything, fixed everything, down to the last lovely object for the last glass case of the last corner, left over, of my old show. That's the only take-off, that it has made us perhaps lazy, a wee bit languid—lying like gods together, all careless of mankind. . . . as if we were sitting about on divans, with pigtails, smoking opium and seeing visions. "Let us then be up and doing"—what is it Longfellow says? That seems sometimes to ring out; like the police breaking in—into our opium-den—to give us a shake. [*Golden Bowl*, 24:90–91, 92]

Adam is not fully alert to the dangers of passivity: he still thinks he *is* "doing," and he takes satisfaction in having "so perfectly contented" Charlotte and in having put her "so at her ease" (24:92). His eyes are opened to the adultery and to the selfishness of the life they all lead, but never to his own sin. He consents to return to American City *for Maggie's sake*—because Maggie tells him that she cannot endure the thought that her selfish attachment to him has deprived him of the chance to live his own life. Maggie thus sets him "free" to take the risk of his own life; but in acting for her, he remains essentially inert as a moral agent. As we have seen, he "circulates" in imitation of the world's motion to the very end.

As for Amerigo, he remains the golden bowl—motionless, inert, flawed. When he sees that Maggie knows about his adultery, he still stands "with his hands in his pockets" (24:187). When she shows him that she believes in his good character, it is she who has "to 'do all,' to go the whole way over, to move indefatigably while he stood as fixed in his place as some statue of one of his forefathers" (24:323). Maggie, tempted to "fold her hands," must "push further." But Amerigo only waits—and urges Maggie to wait (24:295, 351). He cannot move, cannot love, at all. He can only wander in the dusky rooms or "recline on deep sofas and stare before him through the smoke of ceaseless cigarettes"; he is another opium-eater, "resting so from that constant strain of the perfunctory to which he was exposed at Fawns" (24:293, 294). Small wonder that in our last view of the adulterers we see them "seated" at tea, "placed" like furniture, or "sitting as still, to be thus appraised, as a pair of effigies of the contemporary great on one of the platforms of Madame Tussaud" (24:360–61).

They are, in the end, not alive at all. In their total acceptance of the way of the world, they do not morally exist. They are only negative or neutral—"nothing." And that is why Amerigo, the golden bowl, in all his "stupid elegance," asks Maggie, apropos of the marriage-gift, "You received then nothing at all?" And it is also why Maggie, when asked whether she has anything to accuse Charlotte of, replies to Charlotte: "I accuse you—I accuse you of nothing" (24:250).

Thus James's work culminates in his fullest and most penetrating repudiation of the passivity that he felt from earliest childhood to be an affliction of his own personality. And it is perhaps the most impressive testimony to James's freedom of mind, his emancipation from all narrow views, that he thus acknowledged indirectly an affinity between himself and the other passive prisoners in the cage of the material world.

But here a question arises. In contemplating James's many depictions of the world as a cage and of life as "the great trap," the critic may be tempted to view James's work, particularly his later novels, as a wholesale attack upon an unregenerate secularism. At least one perceptive reader of James—Graham Greene—has seen James as moving toward the embrace of a religious faith toward the end of his career.[11] Was he? Certainly there is some evidence to support the contention. For the great evil of James's villains is, as we have seen again and again, their worldliness, their passive surrender to "things as they are." Indeed, James is so determined to underscore this idea that he often identifies his villains with the world. Madame Merle is "the great round world itself"—a "round" and "ample" woman with a "world-wide" smile, one who "knows absolutely everything on earth there is to know" (*Portrait*, 3:289, 276, 277). Osmond's name contains the word *monde*. Prince Amerigo is "round" like the golden bowl and like the world he serves. Miriam Rooth is "constructed to revolve like the terrestrial globe" and made "to parade about the world" (*Tragic Muse*, 8:195, 197). The life of Mrs. Lowder bristles with elements that "represent the world" (*Wings*, 19:170). And James's most passive characters, like Merton Densher and Prince Amerigo, are seen making "revolutions" or "turning" round and round like the earth. Indeed, at the end of *The Golden Bowl*, we see all of society revolving in circles. The doors in Adam Verver's mansion open into "sinister circular passages"; the "bedizened performers of the circus" are "poured into the ring"; Adam Verver is seen "vaguely circulating"; Fanny Assingham makes "slow revolutions" (24:288, 289, 291). The ticking watch of necessity has "brought round" the mornings, evenings, and afternoons in which the unregenerate social animals play cards or chess amid the "slow circulation of precious tinkling jugs" (24:297). T. S. Eliot's vision of a turning world doomed to a meaningless secularism is not, perhaps, very different from James's view of the sphere whose confines "move on even as we ourselves move."

Yet in viewing the world as a cage and unregenerate materialism as an abomination, James was not, I think, suggesting anywhere that secularism is the paramount evil to be extirpated. (The paramount evils in James's fiction are coercion and utter passivity.) Nor can we accept Greene's contention that James was moving toward an embrace of religious faith toward the end of his life.[12] On the contrary, we have seen that James regarded organized religion, at least, as one more trap in a world remorselessly fixed on destruction of the soul's freedom. And if he abhorred unregenerate materialism, he also recognized, like the French naturalists, that it is the product of "necessity" and, from a naturalistic point of view, part of the "innocence" of our material being.

James's obsession with his vision of a world of cages has prompted some critics—Sally Sears and Quentin Anderson are notable examples—to conclude that James's imagination is negative and escapist in its tendencies, that James fails to formulate a positive vision of conduct or to develop a clear and responsible view of individual action in relation to social institutions and the conditions of community life in which responsible conduct must inevitably be carried on. It is freedom from the world that James keeps talking about; but to talk about "freedom from," it is argued, is idle unless one also suggests that there is, for the individual, a responsible alternative to the cage. James's whole aim, says Anderson, is to substitute the "imperial self" for the world; and, he concludes, that substitution is romantic escapism, nothing less.

The argument is persuasive; yet it neglects two important elements in James's thought that we have already touched on. In the first place, it is clear that in the later novels—particularly *The Wings of the Dove* and *The Golden Bowl*—James does regard action within the world of institutions and organized social life as necessary. As we have seen, he repudiates the sort of passivity that retreats from a confrontation with evil. And even in the novels written before his major phase—*The Portrait of a Lady, The Bostonians,* and *The Spoils of Poynton*—the escapist tendencies of his heroines are repeatedly subjected to a withering ironic scrutiny.

In the second place, James's vision of human freedom must be seen, I think, in the context of his recognition of the complexity of a world in which "what one has done has been conditioned and related and involved—so to say, fatalised—every element and effort jammed up against some other necessity or yawning over some consequent void. . . . " He saw that to face realistically the complexity of concrete life, we must recognize that action necessarily entails risks: action meant to introduce positive values may produce corresponding losses and negative results. If James keeps talking about freedom, he never ignores the interconnectedness of things and never oversimplifies cause-and-effect relationships; that he leaves to romantic exponents of "freedom." The rationalists' cry for liberty in the French Revolution ignored what James called the "deeper and darker and unapparent [life], in which things *really* happen to us" (*Letters,* 2:105); it neglected the will-to-power and the terrible momentum of the irrational. James has no use for such a romantic version of "liberty." And if his exclamation "Thank God . . . I've no opinions!" sounds irresponsible to those who, in the grip of revolutionary passion, would drown evil in one great sea of blood, James (in *The Princess Casamassima*) recognized that "the ulcer of envy" and the lust for power are inseparable from the desire for justice and social reform. James's "escape from ideas," viewed in this light, is anything but negative or irresponsible; it is, on the contrary, a recognition that ideas, as such, are empty; that, as D. H. Lawrence argued so eloquently, we can go wrong in the mind; that the only freedom human beings can ever enjoy in this world is a freedom for which they must pay a staggering price.

James's recognition of the limitations of "freedom" is pessimistic, to be sure. His imagination is all Sophoclean. But to see the world as a cage need not lead one to despair: authentic freedom exists within the confines of the cage. Like Milly Theale, man may exist in "caged freedom." Only we must have imagination enough to see our freedom for what it is—and to recognize, above all, what it entails. Inauthentic versions of freedom, one might suggest, are the products of men who lack imagination.

6
The Artist's Freedom

In purpose the least doctrinal of critics, it was by his very horror of dogmas, moulds, and formulas, that he so effectively contributed to the science of literary interpretation.

—Henry James on Sainte-Beuve

No study of the adventures of the imagination in James's work would be complete without a glance at James's criticism. For it is no exaggeration to say that the theme of freedom and encagement developed in the fiction is developed with almost equal richness in James's criticism—and that the criticism, too, reflects the preoccupation with action and passivity that we have examined in *A Small Boy and Others*. The key terms in James's criticism, as in his stories, are "living" and "freedom." If active participation in the world is ruled out for men like James, there remains the alternative of "living" indirectly—living by writing. The artist lives too; indeed, he lives intensely, lives by creating, by letting himself go, by doing as much as possible with the allotted gifts within the allotted time. His religion is "the religion of doing." And his happy fate, as James says in "The Lesson of Balzac," is "to *partake* of life, actively, assertively, not passively, narrowly, in mere sensibility and sufferance. . . . "[1] In reaching out, in assimilating as much of life as possible, in refusing to allow his "grasping imagination" to be confined or intimidated, the artist finds an unprecedented freedom, an unprecedented enlargement of consciousness, and a life that was to James—for all the penalties attached to it, all the austerities and renunciations —a gift of the gods:

151

Here lurks an immense homage to the general privilege of the artist, to that constructive, that creative passion—portentous words, but they are convenient—the exercise of which finds so many an occasion for appearing to him the highest of human fortunes, the rarest boon of the gods. He values it, all sublimely and perhaps a little fatuously, for itself—as the great extension, great beyond all others, of experience and of consciousness; with the toil and trouble a mere sun-cast shadow that falls, shifts and vanishes, the result of his living in so large a light. . . . It may leave him weary and worn; but how, after his fashion, he will have lived! As if one were to expect at once freedom and ease! That silly safety is but the sign of bondage and forfeiture.[2]

The artist lives the largest possible life because, in his daring, he enjoys the greatest possible extension of experience and consciousness. The freest life is the largest life, the largest the freest: life unconfined to a single perspective. Freedom is expansion, flexibility; it is the recognition of "Variety, variety,"[3] a happy pluralism, being as complete and wide-ranging as possible. Everything is open to the artist. As James says in "The Art of Fiction": "It appears to me that no one can ever have made a seriously artistic attempt without becoming conscious of an immense increase—a kind of revelation—of freedom. One perceives in that case—by the light of a heavenly ray—that the province of art is all life, all feeling, all observation, all vision."[4]

Of all free spirits the novelist is, perhaps, the most fortunate. For the novel is pre-eminently freedom's vehicle—it is "of all pictures the most comprehensive and the most elastic. It will stretch anywhere—it will take in absolutely everything" (*HF*, pp. 50–51). "It can do simply everything, and that is its strength and its life. Its plasticity, its elasticity are infinite; there is no colour, no extension it may not take from the nature of its subject or the temper of its craftsman. . . . it moves in a luxurious independence of rules and restriction." (*HF*, p. 53). "The other arts, in comparison, appear confined and hampered; the various conditions under which they are exercised are so rigid and definite. But the only condition that I can think of attaching to the composition of the novel is, as I have already said, that it be sincere" (*PP*, p. 407). So free is the novelist that his duty is simply "to be as complete as possible."

This desire to express his freedom by grasping the maximum of reality is one of James's constant concerns, not only in his criticism but also in his development of his fiction. He wished to "put all that is possible" of his animating idea "into a form and compass that will contain and express it"—to make his production "bristle" with life, life as thick and dense as "the rich density of wedding-cake" (*AN*, pp. 87–88). But the artist setting out to pack as much life as possible into his work is inevitably confronted by tremendous problems. As Gabriel Nash observes in *The Tragic Muse*, "The book of life's padded, ah but padded—a deplorable want of editing" (8:26). Art has a way of resisting the diversity and variety of life. The artist abstracts ruthlessly, and all of life is bent to his artistic purposes. He cuts, splices, rearranges, simplifies, distorts, and casts out any materials that threaten to mar the perfection of the artistic whole. How then can one talk about the "truth" and "reality" of the representation of life? The problem fascinated James, and we see him returning again and again in his criticism to the tug-of-war between the idea and the swarming reality, between art and life. "Life being all inclusion and confusion, and art being all discrimination and selection," what are the "primary laws for a saving selection" (*AN*, p. 120)— a selection that rescues life from its "splendid waste" and yet does no violence to the essential complexity, the "terrible mixture" in things?

The means by which the novelist "saves" life—the maximum quantity of it—are explored in a hundred passages of James's criticism. We may single out three important aspects of his solution to the problem of wedding reality to art: first, the selection of materials; second, "execution," including such matters as characterization, plotting, and diction; third, the artist's state of mind in the act of composition. As we shall see, James held that the greatest creators are the freest men, those who have overcome the limitations of their backgrounds and are able to rise above cultural and temperamental biases. The creator has to be free if he would create that large, impersonal correspondence with life that has the dignity and authority of a work by a historian or a scientist; and as James says in his essay on Trollope, "It is only as an historian that [the novelist] has the smallest *locus standi*" (*PP*, p. 116). Particularly in an age in which the art of fiction had become practically "a bankrupt and discredited art," James felt it was necessary to protest against the factitious, against easy improvisations, easy importations into the novel of the "accidental and the arbitrary" by the "loose and easy producers, the great resounding improvisatori" (*HF*, p. 65)—especially against the introduction of material gratuitous in the sense that it does not arise from the *donnée* with which the creator begins. The logic of the novel must be no mere logic of improvisation, James argued; nor must the image of life be merely an expression of the artist's personality. The novel must have, rather, all the exactitude and must reflect all the scrupulous detachment of a scientific work. It must be an image of life, not an image of the artist's soul.

Of immense importance to the "lovers of the image of life" is the selection of materials. "Art is essentially selection," James writes, "but it is a selection whose main care is to be typical, to be inclusive" (*PP*, p. 398). For James the triumph of a novel like *Madame Bovary* is "that Emma interests us by the nature of her consciousness and the play of her mind, thanks to the reality and beauty with which those sources are invested. It is not only that they represent *her* state; they are so true, so observed and felt, and especially so shown, that they represent the state, actual or potential, of all persons like her, persons romantically determined."[5] Flaubert's art thus approaches the symbolic: the universal is dissolved in the particular. It was a similar aspect of Ibsen's art, "the mingled reality and symbolism," that James came to admire;[6] and it was precisely the sort of thing he tried to do in constructing his own symbolism. Yet even where symbolism is absent, one of the greatest virtues of a writer is his selection of material from the center of daily life—from what Wallace Stevens calls "things as they are." Thus, for James, the "great," the "inestimable merit" of Trollope is "a complete appreciation of the usual" (*PP*, pp. 100–101). Similarly, the beauty of Turgenev's writing is that of "the finest presentation of the familiar," and the Russian master's created "air" is that of "the great central region of passion and motive, of the usual, the inevitable, the intimate—the intimate for weal or woe" (*HF*, pp. 171, 172). Small wonder then that James was proud of having written the scene in which Isabel Archer, in a silent "vigil of searching criticism," arrives at an "impression" of the relationship between Madame

Merle and Osmond—arrives at it "without her being approached by another person and without her leaving her chair." Such occasions, the quiet moments when nothing is stirring but imagination and feeling, are characteristic; an art that seeks to grasp reality cannot avoid them. And that is one reason James experimented with [the] story in which "nothing happens," as in "The Story in It" and "The Beast in the Jungle." For like James Joyce, he felt that nothing is more usual than not having adventures; and if Flaubert could write (in *Un coeur simple*) the story of a servant-girl's devotion to a parrot (*PP*, p. 395) a new field is opened to the lover of the image of life: that is, prodigious inaction and unadventurousness.

It is said that James's characters are too cerebral and that they experience, in their well-mannered drawing-room lives, none of the great, the real upheavals of the soul. Where, critics ask, is a Svidrigailov, a Vautrin, a Manfred? But while James was not well acquainted with the lower depths or the underground or the abberrant, his reply to those critics might well have been to counter: where, after all, do most men live? In the age of the bourgeois, a novelist seeking to represent reality must write about *des choses bourgeoises.* As James says in his essay on Maupassant,

> The greater part of [French fiction]—almost all the work of Zola and of Daudet, the best of Flaubert's novels, and the best of the brothers De Goncourt—treat of that vast, dim section of society which, lying between those luxurious walks on whose behalf there are easy presuppositions and that darkness of misery which, in addition to being picturesque, brings philanthropy also to the writer's aid, constitutes really, in extent and expressiveness, the substance of any nation. In England, where the fashion of fiction still sets mainly to the country house and the hunting-field, and yet more novels are published than anywhere else in the world, that thick twilight of mediocrity of condition has been little explored. May it yield triumphs in the years to come! [*PP*, pp. 283–84]

In moving from the "ghostly" materials of *The Portrait of a Lady* to the depiction of the struggle for existence as reflected in ordinary lives—in the life of a Fleda Vetch, a girl in the postal-telegraph office, a Kate Croy or Merton Densher, a Charlotte Stant, a Beale Farange—James hoped himself to explore (and explore extensively) that thick "twilight of mediocrity of condition."

If the novelist, seeking a "complete representation" of life, has gathered his materials from the vast area of the usual, there remains the tremendous task of execution. There are problems of dramatizing, of point of view, of plotting, of characterization, of authorial comment; and there are problems involving tone, perspective, and the proper attitude to be taken by the artist toward his materials. In all his reasonings on these matters, James presses towards a solution to the central problem of reconciling reality's complexity with the ruthless abstracting tendency of art. He continually seeks the rhetoric of fiction that is indistinguishable from life's odd "rhetoric."

Critics who have discussed James's much-heralded use of a central intelligence and his virtual elimination from fiction of the omniscient narrator have stressed repeatedly the aesthetic gains of James's method. The method is more dramatic; it produces a more convincing illusion; and so on. But in solving his aesthetic problems, James never forgot his aim of packing the maximum amount of "reality" into his novels. The whole truth about reality may be accessible only to an infinite mind, but human beings can enlarge their views of things, multiply their perspectives, assimilate larger quantities of factual detail, and so arrive at an approximation of "the whole truth." But to do this we must obviously expand our imagination of things. And there are two major ways of effecting such an expansion: one can view the reality in question from a number of different points of view; or one can place at the center of the composition an extremely large and flexible intelligence which comprehends, in its largeness, a variety of points of view.

The use of a number of different perspectives so as to provide, in effect, the whole plurality of truths—the whole truth being, presumably, the sum of all the partial perspectives—always fascinated James. We find him considering the problem in his Preface to *The Tragic Muse:* "What has become," he asks, " . . . of the famous centre of one's subject? It is surely not in Nick's consciousness—since why, if it be, are we treated to such an intolerable dose of Sherringham's? It can't be in Sherringham's—we have for that altogether an excess of Nick's. How on the other hand can it be in Miriam's? . . . " (7:xiv). And after raising this question, which he finds nothing less than "delightful," he answers, with immense pleasure, that the novel is done through a method of "alternation":

> This imposes a consistency other than that of the novel at its loosest, and, for one's subject, a different view and a different placing of the centre. The charm of the scenic consistency, the consistency of the multiplication of *aspects,* that of making them amusingly various, had haunted the author of "The Tragic Muse" from far back, and he was in due course to yield to it all luxuriously, too luxuriously perhaps, in "The Awkward Age." . . . [*Tragic Muse,* 7:xv]

To see Miriam Rooth, the "absolutely objective Miriam," from the points of view of both Sherringham and Nick Dormer—the "exposed subjectivity all around her"—is to see a larger or richer truth than, say, that in Anatole France's "inimitable *Histoire Comique*": "I think I saw Miriam, and without a sacrifice of truth, that is of the particular glow of verisimilitude I wished her most to benefit by, in a complexity of relations finer than any that appear possible for the gentry of M. Anatole France" (7:xvii).

A similar gain is achieved in *The Awkward Age,* in which, despite the thoroughly dramatic method, James feels he has solved the problem that besets the dramatist: the problem of being condemned to utter simplicity and superficiality. "The disdainers of the contemporary drama deny," James points out, " . . . that the matter to be expressed by its means—richly and successfully expressed that is—*can* loom with any largeness; since from the moment it does one of the conditions breaks down" (9:xviii).

But while accepting the conditions of the drama, while employing a purely scenic method (each scene like a lamp that sheds its unique light on the central subject), while thus shutting himself up "wholly to cross-relations, relations all within the action itself; no part of which is related to anything but some other part," James feels that he has not condemned himself to the bareness and simplicity of the drama "I saw the point of my game all in the problem of keeping these conditioned relations crystalline at the same time that I should, in emulation of life, consent to their being numerous and fine and characteristic of the London world (as the London world was in this quarter and that to be deciphered)" (*AN*, p. 114). What James delights in here is what he finds in Browning's *The Ring and the Book*: the "power to scrutinize life from a 'point of view . . . almost sublime' and to 'smuggle' as many 'points of view together into that one' as he wished."[7] Any increase in the number of points of view, any "multiplication of aspects," has the effect of enlarging the novel, and James, always emulous of Balzac's "huge distributed, divided and subdivided picture" of life,[8] avers, in his Preface to *The Tragic Muse*, that he has "put himself . . . as much as possible under the protection" of this method (7:xv).

But his more usual practice was to provide a single "usurping consciousness" from whose point of view everything is seen. The interpreter or "reflector" may be a consciousness limited or large, one narrowed down by ignorance or inexperience or temperamental predilections, or one "subject to fine intensification and wide enlargement" (*AN* p. 62). Clearly, to "get the most" out of life, the novelist must provide, in one way or another, some equivalent of a wide-ranging, imaginative intelligence. As James says in his Preface to *The Princess Casamassima*, apropos of his creation of Hyacinth Robinson:

> . . . I confess I never see the *leading* interest of any human hazard but in a consciousness (on the part of the moved and moving creature) subject to fine intensification and wide enlargement. It is as mirrored in that consciousness that the gross fools, the headlong fools, the fatal fools play their part for us—they have much less to show us in themselves. The troubled life mostly at the centre of our subject—whatever our subject, for the artistic hour, happens to be—embraces them and deals with them for its amusement and its anguish: they are apt largely indeed, on a near view, to be all the cause of its trouble. This means, exactly, that the person capable of feeling in the given case more than another of what is to be felt for it, and so serving in the highest degree to *record* it dramatically and objectively, is the only sort of person on whom we can count not to betray, to cheapen or, as we say, give away, the value and beauty of the thing. By so much as the affair matters *for* some such individual, by so much do we get the best there is of it, and by so much as it falls within the scope of a denser and duller, a more vulgar and more shallow capacity, do we get a picture dim and meagre.

The great chroniclers have clearly always been aware of this;

they have at least always either placed a mind of some sort—in the sense of a reflecting and colouring medium—in possession of the general adventure . . . or else paid signally, as to the interest created, for their failure to do so. [5:xii–xiii]

If one is to give the "maximum sense of what befalls" the troubled center of the composition (*AN*, p. 62), James writes, that center must have a large consciousness and sensibility. He must be "free" precisely in the sense that his consciousness and sensibility are large—are not narrowed down to a merely single-minded view of things. Flaubert, setting himself to deal with the contracted world of Emma Bovary, fails, in James's estimation, because he has provided "such limited reflectors and registers" that "we are forced to believe it to have been by a defect of his mind" (*NN*, p. 64). James, when he undertook in composing *The Spoils of Poynton* to solve a problem similar to Flaubert's, created a consciousness quite as romantic as Emma Bovary's, yet much more complex: an idealizing, sentimentalizing consciousness that is shot through, and all unwittingly, by rapacity and the will-to-power. James's Fleda Vetch can "register" adequately the message of the spoils—all the poetry of them, unless that poetry should turn out to be nothing more, at bottom, than the bleakest prose. Fleda tries unsuccessfully to maintain two opposite views of her situation: an idealized view and a practical, acquisitive view. Emma Bovary is so thoroughly limited to an exclusively romantic vision of life that James must challenge Flaubert's "scale of importances." James characteristically sought to endow his "free spirit" with a divided consciousness and, indeed, to work up interest in his free spirit by contrasting him with the "fools" who have only a single perspective on life.

It is thus as a realist, determined to incorporate the maximum of reality into his fictional world, that James insists on the role of the sensitive central intelligence. To be sure, the artistic reasons for the employment of the central intelligence are compelling. But any comprehensive recording of the happenings of life can be made only by a rich and sensitive "register"—and James was determined to be comprehensive.[9]

His thought about plotting reflects the same insistence on the maximum grasp of truth. The aim is to catch "the very note and trick, the strange, irregular rhythm of life. . . . In proportion as in what she offers us we see life *without* rearrangement do we feel that we are touching the truth; in proportion as we see it *with* arrangement do we feel that we are being put off with a substitute, a compromise and convention" (*PP,* p. 398). There are, for example, no neat endings: life goes on. Isabel Archer returns to Osmond; there is no joyous emancipation with all the fifes and trombones tooting. Lambert Strether loses—and wins; Milly Theale turns her face to the wall—and triumphs; Maggie Verver wins—if she does not lose. But James does not drop plot altogether. In truth, no one works more deliberately with plotted peripeteia, with complications, preparations, warnings, climaxes. (Lawrence Holland has observed that *The Sacred Fount* parodies the schematizing, formalizing, abstracting "method at the heart of the madness.")[10] No artist ever took greater care to impose a unified vision on his fictional world. But James was determined to rescue reality from the artist's mad schematizing in two ways: by thoroughly "doing" his subject, and by insisting upon organic development of the "germ."

To "do" a subject thoroughly is to nurture the whole development from the germ: the interconnectedness of action and reaction, motive and response, the whole conditioned and related state of things; for example, the passivity which, in the fateful network of relations, has the force of action; or the violent action which, hedged round by nullifying circumstances, has the effect of inaction; or the innocence which becomes, in the chain of cause and effect, indistinguishable from evil; or the evil which becomes, or is, innocence. Whatever happens in the novel, the "quality of truth" must be "independent of everything but the subject, but the idea itself" (*HF,* p. 175). The germ grows by its own laws, and the growth may not be prescribed in advance by any of the stale formulae of fiction. Art, in James's words, must fly "in the face of a presumption" (*PP,* p. 395). The disinterested artist, not wishing to impose his opinions on life, but wishing only to see life in its wholeness, never sacrificing the essential richness of the concrete diversity to his idea, such a creator arrives at a higher truth, perhaps, than any single science, acting within its own discipline, can claim. And while the artist's idea shapes the reality it encompasses, it is in turn shaped by life. The artist does not, then, so much impose as he discovers; he lets life speak through him, and the novel becomes, as Laurence Holland has observed, a "searching experiment," not "a demonstration of experience already tested but the searching experiment itself."[11]

From this point of view, it would seem idle to talk about morality and moral judgments in connection with the art of fiction. "The essence of moral energy," James asserts in "The Art of Fiction," "is to survey the whole field." (*PP*, p. 406). It is not that moral distinctions are lost in a fiction that sets out to give a complete representation of reality. It is rather that they are gathered up into something richer than morality: the spectacle of life and process and the interconnectedness of events. Whitehead's observation that science is inevitably falsified by a "myth of isolation"—the myth that any fact may be dealt with in isolation from the total interconnectedness of things—would surely have been important to James, for it provides a prime justification for using the words "reality" and "truth" in any consideration of fiction.

James's reasoning about the state of mind of the creator reflects a similar concern with truth and reality. One of the chief conditions for creating a "complete representation" of life is that the novelist free himself insofar as he is able from the chains of his temperament, his culture, his time. Neither the optimist nor the pessimist, for example, can do justice to the complexity of life: both limit the field too severely.

In England, James writes, there is "a perpetual quest for pleasantness" in fiction. The Victorian concession to "the young" has produced "an immense omission in our fiction": the "love-making" has simply been left out (*HF*, p. 56). And, as James remarks icily, "It must never be forgotten that the optimism of that literature is partly the optimism of women and of spinsters; in other words the optimism of ignorance as well as of delicacy" (*PP*, p. 273). James notes that the fierce "struggle for existence" is neglected by good-humored English authors. Yet the French are equally limited by their pessimism: they lack "a large experience of the positive kind," "good humor," and "a general friendliness of conception about our possibilities" (*PP*, pp. 273–74). The "extraordinary effort" of the great Zola, James writes, is "vitiated by a spirit of pessimism on a narrow basis. M. Zola is magnificent, but he strikes an English reader as ignorant; he has an air of working in the dark; if he had as much light as energy, his results would be of the highest value" (*PP*, p. 408). Moreover, James deplores Zola's lack of wit—and "what tricks the absence of a sense of it plays him! . . . Is it not also owing to the absence of a sense of humor that this last and most violent expression of the realistic faith [*Nana*] is extraordinarily wanting in reality?" (*HF*, p. 279). James finds a similar limitation in Flaubert. Was Flaubert "absolutely and exclusively condemned to irony?" he asks. "The 'gift' was of the greatest, a force in itself, in virtue of which he is a consummate writer; and yet there are whole sides of life to which it was never addressed and which it apparently quite failed to suspect as a field of exercise" (*NN*, p. 76). As for Maupassant, James concludes that his ironic spirit is so finely honed that he is incapable of creating "disciplined manhood" and he skips the "whole reflective part of his men and women—that reflective part which governs conduct and produces character." James grants Maupassant his freedom to limit the field; but he cannot forbear commenting, "No wonder you have a contempt if that is the way you limit the field. . . . Your work, on your premises, remains the admirable thing it is, but is your 'case' not adequately explained?" (*PP*, pp. 285–86).

The English, James concludes, have chosen to stress mind or soul, the French to stress instinct and passion. Zola "had to leave out the life of the soul, practically, and confine himself to the life of the instincts, of the more immediate passions. . . . " (*HF*, p. 75). Maupassant "judges life only from the point of view of the senses" (*PP*, p. 254). Flaubert chooses, as "special conduits" of the life he wishes to depict, "inferior" and "abject human specimens": Emma Bovary and Frédéric Moreau, both too poor for their parts, their consciousnesses too impoverished to reflect adequately the actual complexity and richness of life (*NN*, pp. 65–66). But if the French have not sufficiently stressed the reflective part of human nature, James is very far from wishing, as a counterbalance, an emphasis on mind or spirit. On the contrary, in life there is only the spirit encumbered by conditions, by matter. To cut the spirit off from conditions is to indulge in the most irresponsible romanticism—that is, "experience liberated . . . disengaged, disembroiled, disencumbered, exempt from the conditions that we usually know to attach to it. . . . " (*AN*, p. 33).

But in a great artist such as Balzac, who has mastered "the art of complete representation," James is struck by "the part assigned by him, in any picture, to the *conditions* of the creatures with whom he is concerned. Contrasted with him other prose painters of life scarce seem to see the conditions at all" (*HF*, p. 80). Thus James's final answer to those who would place him in the camp either of tough-minded physical reductionists or of tender-minded idealists is that he refuses to be placed in either. As he says in his letter of 1889 to the Deerfield Summer School, neither "materializing tendencies" nor "spiritualizing" nor "etherealizing" tendencies are meaningful to the novelist: "There are no tendencies worth anything but to see the actual or the imaginative, which is just as visible, and to paint it. I have two little words for the matter remotely approaching to rule or doctrine; one is life and the other freedom" (*FN*, p. 29).

But the rejection of pessimism or optimism, of an emphasis on matter or mind, is hardly enough. The artist who would master the art of complete representation must reject the tendentious in whatever form it threatens to vitiate the image of life. And that, finally, is why James prefers, over the limited vision of tragedy or of comedy, a complex fusion that renders the true diversity of life. I have dealt briefly elsewhere with the tragicomic nature of James's art;[12] here it will be useful to repeat and amplify some of those earlier remarks.

Ellen Leyburn's excellent study *Strange Alloy* calls our attention to the "mingled tragedy and comedy of life" in James's work and argues persuasively that James's career is marked by an effort to do away with comedy and tragedy as "separable" elements in his fiction. In the early work, Leyburn writes, comedy remains "separable, an element used for the specific purposes of contrast, satiric definition of the sources of evil, or affectionate mockery"; "in the late novels the comedy has become also an inseparable part of the tragic experience of the characters who even on the edge of the abyss find their 'consciousness interesting.' "[13] She also finds in James's use of fools who are often pathetic, of partly tragic minor characters, and of "free spirits," an attempt to render the mingled tragedy and comedy of life. And she might have carried her argument even further, I believe. For while it is roughly true that Lambert Strether (for example) is "tragically involved" and also "comically detached enough to see the incongruity [of his situation] as comic," it is perhaps more to the point that Strether is viewed both sympathetically and ironically by James. Strether is a hero, to be sure, but with his bright nippers bestriding his nose, his timid gaze, and his inveterate "Do I dare?," he is second cousin to J. Alfred Prufrock. James was determined to resist the moralistic view which divides mankind into two camps, the good and the wicked. If romance thrives on the convention of the "rank vegetation of the 'power' of bad people that good get into" (*AN*, p. 37), in James's art (although its melodramatic structure often leads readers to see a simple division of the "bad" from the "good") simple moral distinctions tend to dissolve in the recognition that virtue and vice commingle and that, as T. S. Eliot writes in *Gerontion*,

> Unnatural vices
> Are fathered by our heroism. Virtues
> Are forced upon us by our impudent crimes.

Especially as James's fiction reaches its maximum complexity, the "bad" people turn out to be creatures like Charlotte Stant or Kate Croy, whose "evil" is their "necessity"—their daily worldliness, normal acquisitiveness, normal desire. Nor are there any heroes in James's work who are seen without irony and a view of their motives that is often, in the last analysis, devastating. Maggie Verver is a saint, a redeemer, but she's also a cunning little manipulator, a dismal nun, and a bore. Fleda Vetch is a high priestess at the altar of the ideal—and a leech, an avid profit-seeker with an eye on the Spoils.

Thus when James says, in the much-quoted passage in his Preface to *The Spoils of Poynton*, that the tormented "free spirit" in his works is "heroic, ironic, pathetic or whatever," (10:xv), he means that the free spirit is all of these in combination—both hero and anti-hero, in short a real human being. Or as he observed, when asked by Henry Harper to write a story on American snobbishness abroad, "But the only way that's at all luminous to look at it is to see what there may be in it of most eloquent, most illustrative and most human—most characteristic and essential: what is its real, innermost, dramatic, tragic, comic, pathetic, ironic note," (*Notebooks*, p. 176). The evidence is indeed overwhelming that throughout his career, both in constructing his characters and in plotting their fortunes, James was very deliberately seeking to achieve a sort of "balance and reconciliation of discordant qualities." The passage from which Leyburn takes the title of her study is only one of many eloquent passages that might be cited to show that James's determination was to "reflect for us, out of the confusion of life, the close connexion of bliss and bale, of the things that help with the things that hurt, so dangling before us for ever the bright hard medal, of so strange an alloy, one face of which is somebody's right and ease and the other somebody's pain and wrong" (*AN* p. 143).

It is not surprising, then, that James's highest praise goes to those artists who represent the "terrible mixture" in things. The greatness of Balzac, for example, consists to a very great extent for James in "the mixture of sun and shade diffused through the *Comédie Humaine*—a mixture richer and thicker and representing an absolutely greater quantity of 'atmosphere' than we shall find prevailing within the compass of any other suspended frame" (*HF*, pp. 71–72). James finds the same sovereign mixture in the work of Daudet: as Lawrence Holland has observed, "James had discovered in Daudet a complex fusion which he thought 'modern': a combination of ingratiating 'sociability' and 'light comicality' with the depiction of 'the miseries and cruelties of life.' "[14] Maupassant, at his best, exhibits a similar distinction: "The breadth, the freedom, and brightness of [*La Maison Tellier*]," James writes, ". . . give the measure of the author's talent, and of that large, keen way of looking at life which sees the pathetic and the droll, the stuff of which the whole piece is made, in the queerest and humblest patterns" (*PP*, p. 269). Even more eloquent is James's praise of Turgenev, whose magnificence is to be found in the extraordinary completeness of his vision, in the combination of the ironic and the tender, of "reality" and poetry, in the extraordinary sense of "fate and folly and pity and wonder and beauty":

> No one has had a closer vision, or a hand at once more ironic and more tender, for the individual figure. He sees it with its minutest signs and tricks—all its heredity of idiosyncrasies, all its particulars of weakness and strength, of ugliness and beauty, of oddity and charm; and yet it is of his essence that he sees it in the general flood

of life, steeped in its relations and contacts, struggling or submerged, a hurried particle in the stream. This gives him, with his quiet method, his extraordinary breadth; dissociates his rare power to particularize from dryness or hardness, from any peril of caricature. He understands so much that we almost wonder he can express anything; and his expression is indeed wholly in absolute projection, in illustration, in giving of everything the unexplained and irresponsible specimen. He is of a spirit so human that we almost wonder at his control of his matter; of a pity so deep and so general that we almost wonder at his curiosity. The element of poetry in him is constant, and yet reality stares through it without the loss of a wrinkle. No one has more of that sign of the born novelist which resides in a respect unconditioned for the freedom and vitality, the absoluteness when summoned, of the creatures he invokes. . . . [*HF*, pp. 173–74]

And if this marvelous admixture of the tragic with the comic, the ironic with the tender, the individual figure with the conditions of his life, and the poetic with the realistic is found in the great novelist, it is also found in the greatest painters, since painters too are engaged in the difficult business of representing life. Thus in Tintoretto, James finds precisely the same fusion of poetry and reality, the same comprehensive grasp of life, as that in Balzac and Turgenev. In Tintoretto, "the eternal problem of the conflict between idealism and realism dies the most natural of deaths. In his genius the problem is practically solved; the alternatives are so harmoniously interfused that I defy the keenest critic to say where one begins and the other ends. The homeliest prose melts into the most ethereal poetry—the literal and the imaginative fairly confound their identity."[15] Like Balzac, Tintoretto puts a prodigious "quantity of life" into his work. Of his *Crucifixion* James says: "Surely no single picture in the world contains more of human life; there is everything in it, including the most exquisite beauty. It is one of the greatest things of art; it is always interesting."[16]

James's insistence on the admixture of the light and the dark, of bliss and bale, of tragedy and comedy, is finally inseparable from his profound appreciation of the virtue of detachment—a virtue that Meister Eckhardt placed above love in his catalogue of the virtues. As James writes in 1911 to H. G. Wells,

There is, to my vision, no authentic, and no really interesting and no *beautiful*, report of things on the novelist's, the painter's part unless a particular detachment has operated, unless the great stewpot or crucible of the imagination, of the observant and recording and interpreting mind in short, has intervened and played its part. ... [*Letters*, 2:181–82]

Hates and loves—those "fine primitive passions"—"*lose* them-"selves for me," he says, "in the act of contemplation, or at any rate in the act of reproduction" (*Letters*, 2:9). Like his father, James eschews "all sickening partisanship"; the novelist was proud that he had become "as little provincial as possible" (*Notes ... Brother*, p. 170; *Letters*, 1:55).

Recognizing "the patches of ambiguity and the abysses of shadow" everywhere in life, aware that "everything's terrible . . . in the heart of man," James seems sometimes, in his detachment, to have absolved himself even of the responsibility to make moral judgments (*Letters*, 1:289; *Golden Bowl*, 24:349). (We have noted that, in 1898 at least, he said that he had "no *opinions*," "no policy," "no judgment"—that he was "too lost in the mere spectacle for any decent morality" [*Letters*, 1:310, 305, 309].) Yet his detachment and his freedom from partisanship were never really negative, and those who would argue that the morality of James's last novels remains "irreducibly ambiguous"[17] forget, I think, that while James created, after 1883, an ambiguous world—one in which good and evil, selfishness and "innocence," are inseparable—he did not allow this terrible ambiguity of experience to paralyze his moral judgment. Maggie Verver may be guilty of many things; yet even when we have acknowledged her selfishness and her desire to have everything on her own terms, we must recognize that she alone in *The Golden Bowl* has what may be called a sense of sin; she alone strives to break free from the cage of brute appetite and of gilded appearances; she alone accepts responsibility while the others repeatedly disclaim it; she alone has not only "imagination of the states of others" but also when she recognizes the evil she has caused, the desire to undo that evil and to serve "love." Maggie isn't a saint; she wants her Prince and she does what is necessary to seize him. But recognizing the "awful mixture in things," she seeks to devise a solution that, under the circumstances, will be not only just but also expressive of pity and love—a solution that permits the Prince and Charlotte to save face and retain their pride, their dignity, and their places in the world they slavishly adore. Maggie plays the world's game to cheat the world of its fraudulent triumphs. It is precisely this assumption of "the responsibility of freedom"—this working within a world in which good and evil breed each other —that constitutes her redemptive virtue. Whatever her faults, she refuses to yield to worldly wrath; she is detached enough—free enough—to renounce the sordid desire for retaliation and revenge. In the end, she is perhaps as free as anyone can be in a world in which human conduct is "fatalised."

In his darkest moods James could say—with reference to "earthquakes and newspapers and motor-car and aeroplanes"— that he had "lost the desire to live in a situation (by which I mean in a world) in which I can be invaded from so many sides at once" (*Letters*, 2:121). But his pessimism was always qualified by his abiding belief that one can, to a degree, rise above a purely selfish, enslaving world. "Hold up your heart," he writes to Howard Sturgis in 1907,

> and remember, for God's sake, that there is a point beyond which the follies and infirmities of our friends and our *proches* have no right to ravage and wreck our own independence of soul. That quantity is too precious a contribution to the saving human sum of good, of lucidity, and we are responsible for the *entretien* of it. So keep yours, shake yours, up—well up—my dearest friend, and to this end believe in your admirable human use. To be "crushed" is to be of no use; and I for one insist that you shall be of some, and the most delightful, to *me*.   Feel everything, tant que vous voudrez—and *then* soar superior and don't leave tatters of your precious person on every bush that happens to bristle with all the avidities and egotisms. [*Letters*, 2:73]

Trapped in the crystal cage, one can yet soar. In following one's own inclinations, in allowing one's imagination to adventure and speculate, one can smash the crystal and breathe fresh air. In his art, at least, James threw off the fetters of "forfeiture and safety."

Notes

INTRODUCTION

1. Quoted in Leon Edel, *Henry James: The Master, 1901–1916* (Philadelphia: J. B. Lippincott, 1972), pp. 373–74.
2. Ibid., p. 374.
3. *The Novels and Tales of Henry James*, 26 vols. (New York: Charles Scribner's Sons, 1907–17), 15:230–31. Hereafter, unless otherwise indicated, volume and page numbers within the text refer to this (the "New York") edition.
4. In Leon Edel, ed., *Henry James: A Collection of Critical Essays* (Englewood Cliffs, N.J.: Prentice-Hall, 1963), p. 28.
5. Cf. James's remark on Emerson: "He urged that a man should await his call, his finding the thing to do which he should really believe in doing, and not be urged by the world's opinion to do simply the world's work." *Hawthorne* (London: Macmillan, 1879), pp. 82–83.
6. Daniel J. Schneider, *Symbolism: The Manichean Vision* (Lincoln, Neb.: University of Nebraska Press, 1975).
7. The word "image" I would define, following Robert L. Gale, as a "simile or metaphor, in the broadest sense, and not a complex of words evoking a mental picture or a sensory impression." See *The Caught Image: Figurative Language in the Fiction of Henry James* (Chapel Hill: University of North Carolina Press, 1964), p. 4.
8. I am indebted to Elder Olsen for these clear and precise definitions; see his "A Dialogue on Symbolism," in *Critics and Criticism: Ancient and Modern*, ed. Ronald S. Crane (Chicago: University of Chicago Press, 1952), pp. 567–94.
9. Some readers may note an affinity between my antithetical patterns and the structuralists' "binary oppositions." The affinity is more

169

than coincidental, I think; but my method of reading symbolic works testifies to the centripetal nature of a literary work organized around a central conflict—not to universal habits of the human mind.

10. Gale, *The Caught Image*, pp. 28–31.
11. Ibid., p. 159.

JAMES'S SENSE OF LIFE

1. Henry James, *A Small Boy and Others* (New York: Charles Scribner's Sons, 1913), pp. 175–76; hereafter, *Small Boy* in the text.

2. I touch here obviously on Saul Rosenzweig's thesis in his "The Ghost of Henry James: Revised, with a Postscript, 1962," in Walter Sutton and Richard Foster, eds., *Modern Criticism: Theory and Practice* (New York: Odyssey Press, 1963). I believe that Rosenzweig is probably wrong about the influence of James's father, but his thesis that James suffered from a "profound repression of aggressiveness," an "introversion in which both aggression and sexuality were repressed," seems to me on the whole incontestable. And this inner problem is expressed not only in those tales in which the ego confronts the ghost which is "an apotheosis of the unlived life" but, I think, in all of James's fiction.

3. In a letter to William, written in 1899, Henry observes, "Nothing you tell me gives me greater pleasure than what you say of the arrangements made for Harry and Billy in the forest primeval and the vision of their drawing therefrom experiences of a sort that I too miserably lacked (poor Father!) in my own too casual youth. What I most of all feel, and in the light of it conjure you to keep doing for them, is their being *à même* to contract local saturations and attachments in respect to their *own* great and glorious country, to learn, and strike roots into, its infinite beauty, as I suppose, and variety. Then they won't, as I do now, have to assimilate, but halfheartedly, the alien splendours—inferior ones too, as I believe—of the indigestible midi of Bourget and the Vicomte Melchior de Vogüé. . . . make the boys . . . stick fast and sink up to their necks in everything their *own* countries and climates can give de pareil et de supérieur. Its being that 'own' will double their *use* of it. . . ." *The Letters of Henry James*, ed. Percy Lubbock, 2 vols. (New York: Charles Scribner's Sons, 1920), 1:316; hereafter, *Letters* in the text.

4. Van Wyck Brooks, *The Pilgrimage of Henry James* (New York: E. P. Dutton, 1925), chap. 1.

5. Henry James, *Notes of a Son and Brother* (New York: Charles

Scribner's Sons, 1914), p. 156; hereafter, *Notes . . . Brother* in the text.

6. Joseph A. Ward, however, points out: "The pattern of terrified person finding himself even more terrifying than the hideous monster who confronts him is a buried motif in much of James's fiction, especially the late works." See *The Imagination of Disaster: Evil in the Fiction of Henry James* (Lincoln, Neb.: University of Nebraska Press, 1961), p. 8. Ward takes the counterattack as evidence of the protagonist's monstrous behavior; for example, he sees even Lambert Strether as becoming "a force for evil" (p. 159).

7. Lionel C. Knights, "Henry James and the Trapped Spectator," *Southern Review* 4 (Winter 1939): 602–4.

THE DIVIDED SELF

1. Frederick Willey, in his article "The Free Spirit and the Clever Agent in Henry James," *Southern Review* 2 (Spring 1966): 315–28, points out that the "fool" in James's Preface is "neither comic dupe nor jester. The category applied to *mindless authoritarian passion and intellectualized aggressiveness of all sorts*" (p. 320; emphasis added).

2. R. D. Laing, *The Divided Self: An Existential Study in Sanity and Madness* (New York: Penguin Books, 1965), p. 83; all subsequent references are to this edition.

3. The phrase is William James's in *Varieties of Religious Experience* (New York: Modern Library, 1929), p. 131. James's discussion of "The Sick Soul" demonstrates the "normality" of many so-called schizoid tendencies; see especially the discussion of sane "melancholiacs," pp. 149–58.

4. Sally Sears, *The Negative Imagination: Form and Perspective in the Novels of Henry James* (Ithaca, N.Y.: Cornell University Press, 1968), p. 127.

5. *The American*, 1878 edition, in *Selected Novels of Henry James* (New York: Caxton House, 1946), p .103.

6. Sears, *Negative Imagination*, p. 132.

7. Henry James, *The Bostonians* (New York: Modern Library, [1956]), p. 59; all subsequent references are to this edition.

8. Even Amanda Pynsent and Lady Aurora—both regarded by many critics as unquestionably sympathetic—are treated with irony. Pynnie is so enamoured of nobility that she is determined to make a gentleman of Hyacinth—to form him in the image *she* adores. Lady Aurora, for all her apparent benevolence, has only reacted

against a life she finds "dreary and dreadful" (5:252) and her chief aim, all along, is to get hold of Paul Muniment. When the Princess gets Muniment in her power, Lady Aurora reverts immediately to her old habits and Hyacinth finds her "bedizened," dressed for a party, in her home at Belgrave Square.

9. Among critics who treat Nick Dormer's problems as illustrating the artist's opposition to the "life political, the world of public affairs," see Leon Edel, "Introduction to the Torchbook Edition," *The Tragic Muse* (New York: Harper & Brothers, 1960), pp. ix–xii; Dorothea Krook, *The Ordeal of Consciousness in Henry James* (New York: Cambridge University Press, 1962), p. 64; Frederick W. Dupee, *Henry James* (New York: William Sloane, 1951), p. 162; Quentin Anderson, *The American Henry James* (New Brunswick, N.J.: Rutgers University Press, 1957), pp. 103–4; and Robert Falk, "*The Tragic Muse*: Henry James's Loosest, Baggiest Novel?" in Ray B. Browne and Donald Pizer, eds., *Themes and Directions in American Literature* (Lafayette, Ind.: Purdue University Press, 1969), pp. 148–62.

10. "Introduction to the Torchbook Edition," *The Tragic Muse*, pp. xiv–xvii.

11. Krook, *Ordeal of Consciousness*, p. 319.

12. As Alan H. Roper has pointed out in "The Moral and Metaphorical Meaning of *The Spoils of Poynton*," *American Literature* 32 (May 1960): 182–96.

13. Patrick F. Quinn, "Morals and Motives in *The Spoils of Poynton*," *Sewanee Review* 62 (Autumn 1954): 563–77.

14. Nina Baym, "Fleda Vetch and the Plot of *The Spoils of Poynton*," *PMLA* 84 (January 1969): 102–11.

15. For interpretations of Nanda as an example of "the moral sense" thrust into a world of rapacious adults, see, for example, Edmund Wilson's "The Ambiguity of Henry James" and Joseph Warren Beach's "The Figure in the Carpet" in Frederick W. Dupee, ed., *The Question of Henry James* (London: Allan Wingate, 1957), pp. 192, 117–18; Eben Bass, "Dramatic Scene and *The Awkward Age*," *PMLA* 79 (March 1964): 148–57; and Oscar Cargill, *The Novels of Henry James* (New York: Macmillan, 1961), pp. 269–72.

16. Dupee, *Henry James*, pp. 202, 198.

17. Mrs. Brook is part of the circus, but she's not at all like the others. Her "youth" and "innocence" are contrasted throughout with the age and cynicism surrounding her; she is too decent, too sweet, to be effective in the world. When she says that she "can't help

being good perhaps, if that burden's laid on us," she is speaking simple truth.

18. Henry James, *The Notebooks of Henry James,* ed. F. O. Matthiessen and Kenneth B. Murdock (New York: Oxford University Press, 1947), p. 311; hereafter *Notebooks* in the text.

19. Northrop Frye, *T. S. Eliot* (New York: Barnes and Noble, 1950), pp. 48–49.

WARFARE AND AGGRESSION

1. See Alexander Holder-Barell, *The Development of Imagery and its Functional Significance in Henry James's Novels,* Cooper Monographs, no. 3 (Bern: Francke Verlag, 1959); and Gale, *The Caught Image.* There are several dozen articles and books which contain illuminating comments on James's imagery, but none deal with the imagery in relation to the figure in the carpet.

2. Gale, *The Caught Image,* pp. 283, 83–100; see too the comments of Alan H. Roper, "The Moral and Metaphorical Meaning of *The Spoils of Poynton*"; R. W. Short, "Henry James's World of Images," *PMLA* 68 (December 1953): 943–60; Lotus Snow, " 'A Story of Cabinets and Chairs and Tables': Images of Morality in *The Spoils of Poynton* and *The Golden Bowl*," *Journal of English Literary History* 30 (December 1963): 213–35; and the various observations of Holder-Barell in *The Development of Imagery.*

3. *Washington Square* in *Henry James: Selected Fiction,* ed. Leon Edel (New York, E. P. Dutton, 1964), p. 213; Henry James, *Confidence,* ed. Herbert Ruhm (New York: Grosset & Dunlap, The Universal Library, 1962), p. 19. All subsequent references are to these editions.

4. *The Sacred Fount* in *Henry James, Three Novels,* ed. Tony Tanner (New York: Harper & Row, Perennial Classic, 1968), pp. 441, 374, 371; all subsequent references are to this edition.

5. For a much fuller analysis of Fleda, see my article, "The 'Full Ironic Truth' in James's *The Spoils of Poynton*," *Connecticut Review* 2 (April 1969): 50–66.

6. F. O. Matthiessen, *The James Family* (New York: Alfred A. Knopf, 1947), p. 243.

7. In *The Divided Self* R. D. Laing observes that "utter detachment and isolation are regarded [by the divided self] as the only alternative to a clam- or vampire-like attachment in which the other person's life-blood is necessary for one's own survival, and yet is a threat to one's survival" (p. 53). The vampire motif, developed by James in *The Sacred Fount,* is thus the psychological polarity of

"utter detachment." This psychological explanation of detachment, applied to James, seems to me persuasive—so far as it goes. What is left out is, as we have seen in Chapter 1, the extraordinary example of detachment in James's family, particularly Henry, Sr.'s repudiation of all narrowing pursuits and enslaving creeds. James breathed intellectual detachment from his birth.

THE EYE, APPEARANCES, AND ACTING

1. Matthiessen, *The James Family,* p. 129.
2. Ibid., p. 257.
3. Ibid., pp. 257, 258, 682.
4. Laing, *The Divided Self,* p. 71.
5. Ibid., pp. 83, 75.
6. Ibid., pp. 91, 75.
7. Ibid., pp. 84, 87, 89.
8. Ibid., pp. 109, 112, 113.
9. Ibid., p. 113.
10. Ibid., pp. 180, 184.
11. Ibid., p. 101.
12. Daniel J. Schneider, "The Ironic Imagery and Symbolism of James's *The Ambassadors,*" *Criticism* 9 (Spring 1967): 174–96.

THE CAGE

1. In *Henry James: Selected Fiction,* pp. 297, 319, 332.
2. Joseph Warren Beach and Robert L. Gale, among others, see sexual implications in the imagery of keys and bolts. They are unquestionably there. But the pattern of freedom and enslavement accounts not only for the key-and-bolt images but also for a thousand images scarcely explicable in Freudian terms. The unifying principle of the novel is the threat to the free spirit by an encaging world.
3. Laing, *The Divided Self,* pp. 88, 46.
4. Ibid., p. 46.
5. Ibid., pp. 46–47.
6. Ibid., p. 47.
7. Leon Edel, *Henry James: The Middle Years, 1882–1895* (Philadelphia: J. B. Lippincott, 1962), p. 101.
8. For a detailed analysis of *The Tragic Muse* see my "The Theme of Freedom in James's *The Tragic Muse,*" *The Connecticut Review* 7 (April 1974): 5–15.
9. Walter Isle, *Experiments in Form: Henry James's Novels, 1896–1901* (Cambridge, Mass.: Harvard University Press, 1968), p. 5.

10. Joseph A. Ward argues that "in James's fiction it is nearly axiomatic that the good are reflective and passive, and the evil irreflective and active"; he also argues that evil arises from "the pursuit of good" and is "not an active principle in the universe" as in Manicheism. I think that Ward might have reached a different conclusion had he taken into account James's stress on the connection between passivity and enslavement. Evil—even in the sense in which Ward defines the term—is often nothing less in James's fiction than total surrender to the world, and arises from the pursuit of what the world takes to be good. See *The Imagination of Disaster*, p. 10.

11. Graham Greene, "Henry James: The Religious Aspect," in *The Lost Childhood and Other Essays* (London: William Heinemann, 1951), pp. 31–39.

12. Robert M. Slabey, in his "Henry James and 'The Most Impressive Convention in All History,'" *American Literature* 30 (March 1958): 89–102, argues that James "was drawn to Catholicism for aesthetic reasons and found there many beliefs that consoled him" (p. 92). But the very word *convention* is ominous in much of James's work, and some of the evidence Slabey adduces in support of this opinion might easily, I think, be used to show that James wasn't drawn to Catholicism. F. O. Matthiessen's conclusion about James's religious position—a conclusion supported by Robert L. Gale—seems to me much more satisfactory: "James's religion was phrased very accurately by T. S. Elliot as an 'indifference to religious dogma' along with an 'exceptional awareness of spiritual reality.'" See Matthiessen, *Henry James: The Major Phase* (New York: Oxford University Press, 1944), p. 145; for Gale's remarks, see *The Caught Image*, p. 149.

THE ARTIST'S FREEDOM

1. In *The House of Fiction*, ed. Leon Edel (London: R. Hart-Davis, 1957), p. 73; hereafter *HF* in the text.

2. In *The Art of the Novel: Critical Prefaces by Henry James*, ed. R. P. Blackmur (New York: Charles Scribner's Sons, 1934), pp. 29–30; hereafter *AN* in the text. See also James's passionate statement (*Notebooks*, p. 106): "Try everything, do everything, render everything—be an artist, be distinguished, to the last. . . . I have only to live and to work, to look and to feel, to *gather*, to note. My *cadres* all there; continue, ah, continue, to fill them." By 1904, and probably several years earlier, James felt that he was able to fill his *cadres* with everything in experience. In a 1904 letter to W. D. Howells, he writes: "I am hungry for Material, whatever I may be

moved to do with it; and, honestly, I think, there will not be an inch or an ounce of it unlikely to prove grist to my intellectual and 'artistic' mill" (*Letters*, 2:9).

3. See the earlier comment on his father's "narrowness of exclusion" (*Notes . . . Brother*, pp. 168–69): "Variety, variety—that sweet ideal, *that* straight contradiction of any dialectic. . . . "

4. In *Partial Portraits* (London and New York: Macmillan, 1888), pp. 398–99; hereafter *PP* in the text.

5. *Notes on Novelists with Some Other Notes* (New York: Charles Scribner's Sons, 1914), p. 63; hereafter *NN* in the text.

6. See Leon Edel, *Henry James: The Treacherous Years, 1895–1901* (Philadelphia: J. P. Lippincott, 1969), p. 29.

7. Laurence B. Holland, *The Expense of Vision: Essays on the Craft of Henry James* (Princeton: Princeton University Press, 1964), p. 164.

8. *The Future of the Novel: Essays on the Art of Fiction*, ed. Leon Edel (New York: Random House, Vintage Books, 1956), p. 106; hereafter *FN* in the text.

9. The best "register" in literature, he felt, was Hamlet: it is "prodigious," "the most capacious and most crowded, the moral presence the most asserted, in the whole range of fiction. . . . " (*Art of the Novel*, p. 90).

10. Holland, *The Expense of Vision*, p. 181.

11. Ibid., p. 69.

12. Schneider, *Symbolism: The Manichean Vision*, pp. 113–14.

13. Ellen Douglass Leyburn, *Strange Alloy: The Relation of Comedy to Tragedy in the Fiction of Henry James* (Chapel Hill: University of North Carolina Press, 1968), pp. 171–72.

14. Holland, *The Expense of Vision*, p. 126.

15. Henry James, *Italian Hours* (New York: Horizon Press, 1968), p. 79.

16. Ibid., p. 29.

17. Ruth B. Yeazell, "Talking in James," *PMLA* 91 (January 1976): 77. Yeazell's reply to my argument here may be found in "Forum," *PMLA* 91 (October 1976): 922–24.

Bibliography

Allott, Miriam. "Form versus Substance in Henry James." *Review of English Literature* 3 (January 1962): 53–66.

—————. "Symbol and Image in the Later Work of Henry James." *Essays in Criticism* 3 (July 1953): 321–36.

Anderson, Quentin. *The American Henry James.* New Brunswick, N.J.: Rutgers University Press, 1957.

—————. *The Imperial Self: An Essay in American Literary and Cultural History.* New York: Alfred A. Knopf, 1971.

Andreas, Osborne. *Henry James and the Expanding Horizon.* Seattle: University of Washington Press, 1948.

Auden, W. H. "Henry James and the Artist in America." *Harpers* 197 (July 1948): 36–40.

Bass, Eben. "Dramatic Scene and *The Awkward Age.*" *PMLA* 79 (March 1964): 148–57.

Baym, Nina. "Fleda Vetch and the Plot of *The Spoils of Poynton.*" *PMLA* 84 (January 1969): 102–11.

Beach, Joseph Warren. *The Method of Henry James.* New Haven: Yale University Press, 1918.

Beebe, Maurice. "The Turned Back of Henry James." *South Atlantic Quarterly* 53 (July 1953): 321–36.

Bennett, Joan. "The Art of Henry James: *The Ambassadors.*" *Chicago Review* 9 (Winter 1956): 12–26.

Bethurum, Dorothy. "Morality and Henry James." *Sewanee Review* 31 (July 1923): 324–30.

Bewley, Marius. *The Complex Fate.* New York: Grove Press, 1953.

—————. *The Eccentric Design: Form in the Classic American Novel.* New York: Columbia University Press, 1963.

Blackall, Jean Frantz. *Jamesian Ambiguity and "The Sacred Fount."* Ithaca, N.Y.: Cornell University Press, 1965.

Booth, Wayne C. *The Rhetoric of Fiction*. Chicago: University of Chicago Press, 1961.

Bowden, Edwin T. *The Themes of Henry James*. New Haven: Yale University Press, 1956.

Brooks, Van Wyck. *The Pilgrimage of Henry James*. New York: E. P. Dutton, 1925.

Brown, E. K. "James and Conrad." *Yale Review* 35 (1946): 265–85.

Buitenhuis, Peter. *The Grasping Imagination: The American Writings of Henry James*. Toronto: University of Toronto Press, 1970.

Canby, Henry Seidel. *Turn West, Turn East: Mark Twain and Henry James*. Boston: Houghton Mifflin, 1951.

Cargil, Oscar. *The Novels of Henry James*. New York: Macmillan, 1961.

Cecil, L. Moffit. "Virtuous Attachment in James's *The Ambassadors*." *American Quarterly* 19 (1967): 719–44.

Clair, John A. *The Ironic Dimension in the Fiction of Henry James*. Pittsburgh: Duquesne University Press, 1965.

Conn, Peter J. "The Tyranny of the Eye: The Observer as Aggressor in Henry James's Fictions." Ph.D. dissertation, Yale University, 1969.

Cook, Albert. "The Portentous Intelligent Stillness: James." In *The Meaning of Fiction*, pp. 134–66. Detroit: Wyane State University Press, 1960.

Crews, Frederick C. *The Tragedy of Manners: Moral Drama in the Later Novels of Henry James*. New Haven: Yale University Press, 1957.

Dupee, Frederick W. *Henry James*. New York: William Sloane, 1951.

——————, ed. *The Question of Henry James*. London, Allan Wingate, 1957.

Edel, Leon. "The Architecture of James's New York Edition." *New England Quarterly* 24 (June 1951): 169–78.

——————. "Henry James: The Americano-European Legend." *University of Toronto Quarterly* 36 (1967): 321–24.

——————. *Henry James: The Conquest of London, 1879–1881*. Philadelphia: J. B. Lippincott, 1962.

——————. *Henry James: The Master, 1901–1916*. Philadelphia: J. B. Lippincott, 1972.

——————. *Henry James: The Middle Years, 1882–1895*. Philadelphia: J. B. Lippincott, 1962.

——————. *Henry James: The Treacherous Years, 1895–1901*. Philadelphia: J. B. Lippincott, 1969.

——————. *Henry James: Henry James: The Untried Years, 1843–1870*. Philadelphia: J. B. Lippincott, 1953.

—————, ed. *Henry James: A Collection of Critical Essays.* Engle-wood Cliffs, N.J.: Prentice-Hall, 1963.

Edgar, Pelham. *Henry James: Man and Author.* Boston: Houghton Mifflin, 1927.

Egan, Michael. *Henry James: The Ibsen Years.* London: Vision Press, 1972.

Falk, Robert. *The Victorian Mode in American Fiction, 1865–1885.* East Lansing: Michigan State University Press.

—————. "*The Tragic Muse:* Henry James's Loosest, Baggiest Novel?" In *Themes and Directions in American Literature,* edited by Ray B. Browne and Donald Pizer, pp. 148–62. Lafayette, Ind.: Purdue University Press, 1969.

Feidelson, Charles. "James and the 'Man of Imagination.'" In *Literary Theory and Structure: Essays in Honor of William K. Wimsatt,* by Frank Brady, John Palmer, and Martin Price, pp. 331–52. New Haven: Yale University Press, 1973.

—————. *Symbolism and American Literature.* Chicago: University of Chicago Press, 1953.

Firebaugh, Joseph. "A Schopenhauerian Novel." *Nineteenth-Century Fiction* 13 (December 1958): 177–97.

Gale, Robert L. *The Caught Image: Figurative Language in the Fiction of Henry James.* Chapel Hill: University of North Carolina Press, 1964.

—————. *Plots and Characters in the Fiction of Henry James.* Ham-den, Conn.: Archon Books, 1965.

Geismar, Maxwell. *Henry James and the Jacobites.* Boston: Houghton Mifflin, 1963.

Gibson, Priscilla. "The Uses of James's Imagery: Drama Through Metaphor." *PMLA* 69 (December 1954): 1075–84.

Gordon, Caroline. "Mr. Verver, Our National Hero." *Sewanee Review* 63 (Winter 1955): 29–47.

Gosse, Edmund. "Henry James." In *Aspects and Impressions,* pp. 17–53. New York: Charles Scribner's Sons, 1922.

Greene, Graham. "Henry James: The Religious Aspect." In *The Last Childhood and Other Essays,* pp. 21–50. London: William Heine-mann, 1951.

Grenander, Mary E. "Henry James's Capricciosa: Christina Light in *Roderick Hudson* and *The Princess Casamassima.*" *PMLA* 65 (June 1960): 303–19.

Habegger, Alfred. "Reciprocity and the Market Place in *The Wings of the Dove* and *What Maisie Knew.*" *Nineteenth-Century Fiction* 25 (1971): 455–73.

Hartsock, Mildred. "The Exposed Mind: A View of *The Awkward Age.*" *Critical Quarterly* 9 (1967): 49–59.

Hoffman, Charles G. *The Short Novels of Henry James.* New York: Bookman Associates, 1957.

Hoffman, Frederick J. "Freedom and Conscious Form: Henry James and The American Self." *Virginia Quarterly Review* 37 (Spring 1961) 269–85.

Holder, Alan. *Three Voyagers in Search of Europe: Henry James, Ezra Pound, and T. S. Eliot.* Philadelphia: University of Pennsylvania Press, 1966.

Holder-Barell, Alexander. *The Development of Imagery and its Functional Significance in Henry James's Novels.* Copper Monographs, no. 3. Bern: Francke Verlag, 1959.

Holland, Laurence B. *The Expense of Vision: Essays on the Craft of Henry James.* Princeton: Princeton University Press, 1964.

Hopkins, Viola. "Visual Art Devices and Parallels in the Fiction of Henry James." *PMLA* 76 (December 1961): 561–74.

Horne, Helen. *Basic Ideas of James's Aesthetics as Expressed in the Short Stories Concerning Artists and Writers.* Marburg: Erich Mauersburger, 1960.

Hueffer (Ford), Ford Madox. *Henry James: A Critical Study.* New York: Dodd Mead, 1916.

Hughes, Herbert L. *Theory and Practice in Henry James.* Ann Arbor: University of Michigan Press, 1926.

Isle, Walter. *Experiments in Form: Henry James's Novels, 1896–1901.* Cambridge, Mass.: Harvard University Press, 1968.

James, Henry. *The American.* Boston: Houghton Mifflin, 1877.

——————. *The American Scene.* New York and London: Harper & Row, 1907.

——————. *The Art of the Novel: Critical Prefaces by Henry James.* Edited by R. P. Blackmur. New York: Charles Scribner's Sons, 1934.

——————. *The Complete Plays of Henry James.* Edited by Leon Edel. Philadelphia and New York: J. B. Lippincott, 1949.

——————. *French Poets and Novelists.* London: Macmillan, 1878.

——————. *The Future of the Novel: Essays on the Art of Fiction.* Edited by Leon Edel. New York: Random House, Vintage Books, 1956.

——————. *Hawthorne.* London, Macmillan, 1879.

——————. *The House of Fiction.* Edited by Leon Edel. London: R. Hart-Davis, 1957.

——————. *Italian Hours.* New York: Horizon Press, 1968.

——————. *The Letters of Henry James.* Edited by Percy Lubbock. 2 vols. New York: Charles Scribner's Sons, 1920.

——————. *The Middle Years.* New York: Charles Scribner's Sons, 1917.

——————. *The Notebooks of Henry James.* Edited by F. O. Matthiessen and Kenneth B. Murdock. New York: Oxford University Press, 1947.

——————. *Notes of a Son and Brother.* New York: Charles Scribner's Sons, 1914.

——————. *Notes on Novelists with Some Other Notes.* New York: Charles Scribner's Sons, 1914.

——————. *The Novels and Stories of Henry James: New and Complete Edition.* Edited by Percy Lubbock. 35 vols. London: Macmillan, 1912–28.

——————. *The Novels and Tales of Henry James* (The "New York Edition"). New York: Charles Scribner's Sons, 1907–17 (26 vols.).

——————. *Partial Portraits.* London and New York: Macmillan, 1888.

——————. *The Question of Our Speech. The Lesson of Balzac: Two Lectures.* Boston and New York: Houghton Mifflin, 1905.

——————. *Selected Letters of Henry James.* Edited by Leon Edel. New York: Farrar, Straus & Giroux, 1955.

——————. *A Small Boy and Others.* New York: Charles Scribner's Sons, 1913.

——————. *Within the Rim and Other Essays.* London: William Collins Sons, 1919.

Kelley, Cornelia Pulsifer. *The Early Development of Henry James.* Rev. ed. Urbana, Ill.: University of Illinois Press, 1965.

Kimmey, John L. "*The Princess Casamassima* and the Quality of Bewilderment." *Nineteenth-Century Fiction* 22 (June 1967): 47–62.

Knights, L. C. "Henry James and the Trapped Spectator." *Southern Review* 4 (Winter 1939): 602–4.

Kraft, James. *The Early Tales of Henry James.* Carbondale, Ill. Southern Illinois University Press, 1969.

Kraft, Quentin G. "The Question of Freedom in James's Fiction." *College English* 26 (1965): 372–76, 381.

Krook, Dorothea. *The Ordeal of Consciousness in Henry James.* New York: Cambridge University Press, 1962.

Lebowitz, Naomi. *The Imagination of Loving: Henry James's Legacy to the Novel.* Detroit: Wayne State University Press, 1965.

Levy, Leo B. *Versions of Melodrama: A Study of the Fiction and Drama of Henry James, 1865–1897.* Berkeley: University of California Press, 1957.

Leyburn, Ellen Douglass. *Strange Alloy: The Relation of Comedy to Tragedy in the Fiction of Henry James.* Chapel Hill: University of North Carolina Press, 1968.

Lubbock, Percy. *The Craft of Fiction.* New York: Charles Scribner's Sons, 1921.

Luecke, Sister Jane Marie. "*The Princess Casamassima*: Hyacinth's Fallible Consciousness." *Modern Philology* 60 (May 1963): 274–80.

Marks, Robert. *James's Late Novels: An Interpretation.* New York: William-Frederick Press, 1960.

Matthiessen, F. O. *Henry James: The Major Phase.* New York: Oxford University Press, 1944.

—————. *The James Family.* New York: Alfred A. Knopf, 1947.

McCarthy, Harold T. *Henry James: The Creative Process.* New York: Thomas Voseloff, 1958.

Melchion, Giorgio. "Cups of Gold for the Sacred Fount: Aspects of James's Symbolism," *Critical Quarterly* 7 (Winter 1965): 301–16.

Miller, James E., Jr. "Henry James: A Theory of Fiction." *Prairie Schooner* 45 (1971): 330–56.

—————. "Henry James in Reality." *Critical Inquiry* 2 (Spring 1976): 585–604.

Mull, Donald L. *Henry James's "Sublime Economy": Money as Symbolic Center in the Fiction.* Middletown, Conn.: Wesleyan University Press, 1973.

O'Connor, Frank. "Transitions: Henry James." In *The Mirror in the Roadway: A Study of the Modern Novel,* pp. 223–36. New York: Alfred A. Knopf, 1956.

Olson, Elder. "A Dialogue on Symbolism." In *Critics and Criticism: Ancient and Modern,* edited by Ronald S. Crane, pp. 567–94. Chicago: University of Chicago Press, 1952.

O'Neill, John P. *Workable Design.* Port Washington, N.Y.: Kennikat Press, 1973.

Paterson, John. "The Language of 'Adventure' in Henry James." *American Literature* 32 (November 1960): 291–301.

Poirier, Richard. *The Comic Sense of Henry James: A Study of the Early Novels.* New York: Oxford University Press, 1960.

Poulet, Georges. *The Metamorphoses of the Circle.* Baltimore: Johns Hopkins University Press, 1966.

Pound, Ezra. "Henry James." In *Make It New,* pp. 251–307. New Haven: Yale University Press, 1935.

Powers, Lyall H. *Henry James: An Introduction and Interpretation.* New York: Holt, Rinehart and Winston, 1970.

—————. "Henry James's Antinomies." *University of Toronto Quarterly* 31 (January 1962): 125–35.

—————, ed. *Henry James's Major Novels: Essays in Criticism.* East Lansing: Michigan University Press, 1973.

Putt, S. Gorley. *A Reader's Guide to Henry James.* Ithaca, N.Y.: Cornell University Press, 1966.

Quinn, Patrick F. "Morals and Motives in *The Spoils of Poynton.*" *Sewanee Review* 62 (Autumn 1954): 563–77.

Roberts, Morris. *Henry James's Criticism.* Cambridge, Mass.: Harvard University Press, 1929.

Roper, Alan H. "The Moral and Metraphorical Meaning of *The Spoils of Poynton.*" *American Literature* 32 (May 1960): 182–96.

Rouse, H. Blair. "Charles Dickens and Henry James: Two Approaches to The Art of Fiction." *Nineteenth-Century Fiction* 5 (September 1959): 151–57.

Rowe, John C. "The Symbolization of Milly Theale: Henry James's *The Wings of the Dove.*" *Journal of English Literary History* 40 (1973): 131–64.

Saloman, Roger B. "Realism as Disinheritance: Twain, Howells and James," *American Quarterly* 16 (Winter 1964): 531–44.

Samuels, Charles T. *The Ambiguity of Henry James.* Urbana: University of Illinois Press, 1971.

Sayre, Robert F. *The Examined Self: Benjamin Franklin, Henry Adams, Henry James.* Princeton: Princeton University Press, 1964.

Schneider, Daniel J. "The Divided Self in the Fiction of Henry James." *PMLA* 90 (May 1975): 447–60.

—————. "The 'Full Ironic Truth' in *The Spoils of Poynton.*" *Connecticut Review* 2 (April 1969): 50–66.

—————. "The Ironic Imagery and Symbolism of James's *The Ambassadors.*" *Criticism* 9 (Spring 1967): 174–96.

—————. *Symbolism: The Manichean Vision.* Lincoln, Neb.: University of Nebraska Press, 1975.

—————. "The Theme of Freedom in James's *The Tragic Muse.*" *Connecticut Review* 7 (April 1974): 5–15.

Sears, Sally. *The Negative Imagination: Form and Perspective in the Novels of Henry James.* Ithaca, N.Y.: Cornell University Press, 1968.

Sharp, Sister M. Corona. *The "Confidante" in Henry James: Evolution and Moral Value of a Fiction Character.* Notre Dame, Ind.: University of Notre Dame Press, 1965.

Shine, Muriel G. *The Fictional Children of Henry James.* Chapel Hill: University of North Carolina Press, 1969.

Short, R. W. "Henry James's World of Images." *PMLA* 68 (December 1953): 943–60.

——————. "Some Critical Terms of Henry James." *PMLA* 65 (September 1950): 667–80.

Shulman, Robert. "Henry James and the Modern Comedy of Knowledge." *Criticism* 10 (1968): 41–53.

Slabey, Robert M. "Henry James and 'The Most Impressive Convention in All History.' " *American Literature* 30 (March 1958): 89–102.

Snell, Edwin Marion. *The Modern Fables of Henry James.* Cambridge, Mass.: Harvard University Press, 1935.

Snow, Lotus. "The Disconcerting Poetry of Mary Temple: A Comparison of The Imagery of *The Portrait of a Lady* and *The Wings of the Dove.*" *New England Quarterly* 31 (September 1958): 312–39.

——————. "The Pattern of Innocence through Experience in the Characters of Henry James." *University of Toronto Quarterly* 22 (April 1953): 230–36.

——————. " 'A Story of Cabinets and Chairs and Tables': Images of Morality in *The Spoils of Poynton* and *The Golden Bowl.*" *Journal of English Literary History* 30 (December 1963): 213–35.

Spender, Stephen. *The Destructive Element.* London: Jonathan Cape, 1935.

Stafford, William T., ed. *James's "Daisy Miller": The Story, The Play, The Critics.* New York: Charles Scribner's Sons, 1963.

Stevenson, Elizabeth. *The Crooked Corridor: A Study of Henry James.* New York: Macmillan, 1949.

Stone, Edward. *The Battle of the Books: Some Aspects of Henry James.* Athens, Ohio: Ohio University Press, 1964.

Sutton, Walter, and Foster, Richard, eds. *Modern Criticism: Theory and Practice.* New York, 1963.

Swan, Michael. *Henry James.* London: Arthur Baker, 1952.

Tanner, Tony. "Henry James." In *The Reign of Wonder: Naivety and Reality in American Literature,* pp. 259–335. New York: Cambridge University Press, 1965.

——————. "The Watcher from the Balcony: Henry James's *The Ambassadors.*" *Critical Quarterly* 8 (Spring 1966): 35–52.

——————, ed. *Henry James: Modern Judgments.* London: Macmillan, 1968.

Tintner, Adeline R. "The Spoils of Henry James." *PMLA* 61 (March 1946): 239–51.

Vaid, Krishna Baldev. *Technique in the Tales of Henry James.* Cambridge, Mass.: Harvard University Press, 1964.

Van Ghent, Dorothy. *The English Novel: Form and Function*. New York: Holt, Rinehart and Winston, 1953.

Ward, Joseph A. *The Imagination of Disaster: Evil in the Fiction of Henry James*. Lincoln, Neb.: University of Nebraska Press, 1961.

——————. *The Search for Form: Studies in the Structure of James's Fiction*. Chapel Hill: University of North Carolina Press, 1967.

Watt, Ian. "The First Paragraph in *The Ambassadors:* An Explication." *Essays in Criticism* 10 (July 1960): 250–74.

Wegelin, Christof. *The Image of Europe in Henry James*. Dallas: Southern Methodist University Press, 1958.

——————. "The Rise of the International Novel." *PMLA* 77 (June 1962): 305–10.

Weinstein, Philip M. *Henry James and the Requirements of the Imagination*. Cambridge, Mass.: Harvard University Press, 1971.

West, Rebecca. *Henry James*. London: Nisbet, 1916.

Wiesenfarth, Joseph. *Henry James and the Dramatic Analogy*. New York: Fordham University Press, 1963.

Willey, Frederick. "The Free Spirit and the Clever Agent in Henry James." *Southern Review* 2 (Spring 1966): 315–28.

Woolf, Virginia. "Henry James." In *The Death of the Moth and Other Essays,* pp. 129–55. London: Hogarth Press, 1942.

Wright, Walter J. *The Madness of Art: A Study of Henry James*. Lincoln, Neb.: University of Nebraska Press, 1962.

Yeazell, Ruth B. "Talking in James." *PMLA* 91 (January 1976): 66–77.

Zabel, Morton D. "Henry James: The Act of Life." In *Craft and Character in Modern Fiction,* pp. 114–43. New York: Viking, 1957.

——————. "Introduction." In *The Portable Henry James,* pp. 1–29. New York: Viking, 1951.

Index